Chess Strategy for Kids

Thomas Engqvist

THE PRINCIPLE OF TWO WEAKNESSES

GAMBIT

First published in the UK by Gambit Publications Ltd 2016

Copyright © Thomas Engqvist 2016

ISBN-13: 978-1-910093-87-0
ISBN-10: 1-910093-87-4

DISTRIBUTION:
Worldwide (except USA): Central Books Ltd, 99 Wallis Rd, London E9 5LN, England.
Tel +44 (0)20 8986 4854 Fax +44 (0)20 8533 5821. E-mail: orders@Centralbooks.com

Gambit Publications Ltd, 99 Wallis Rd, London E9 5LN, England.
E-mail: info@gambitbooks.com
Website (regularly updated): www.gambitbooks.com

Edited by Graham Burgess
Typeset by Petra Nunn
All illustrations by Shane D. Mercer
Printed in the USA by Bang Printing, Brainerd, Minnesota

10 9 8 7 6 5 4 3 2 1

Gambit Publications Ltd
Directors: Dr John Nunn GM, Murray Chandler GM, and Graham Burgess FM
German Editor: Petra Nunn WFM

Contents

Introduction

This collection of 50 Smart Strategies deals with strategic ideas in all phases of the game. It is written, and may be read, as a complementary sequel to *Chess Tactics for Kids*, which covered tactical themes. Strategy and tactics are very closely intertwined since the former deals with the question *"What should I do?"* and the latter with the question *"How should I do it?"*

These are the main questions we must ask ourselves every time it is our turn to move. In other words, strategy is the forming of schemes (mini-plans as well as broader plans) while tactics is the execution of those schemes (moves and variations).

I hope that this book will make the fundamental task of finding the correct strategic ideas easier for juniors as well as for club players.

Finally, I am truly grateful to Graham Burgess and Gambit who gave me the opportunity to write a book about my favourite theme in chess – strategy!

PAWN-ISLANDS

Algebraic Notation

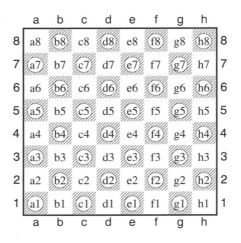

The chess notation used in this book is the simple, algebraic notation in use throughout the world. It can be learnt by anyone in just a few minutes.

As you can see from the chessboard above, the files are labelled a-h (going from left to right) and the ranks are labelled 1-8. This gives each square its own unique reference point. The pieces are described as follows:

Knight = ♘
Bishop = ♗
Rook = ♖
Queen = ♕
King = ♔

Pawns are not given a symbol. When they move, simply the *destination square* is given.

The following additional symbols are also used:

Check	=	+	Good move	=	!
Double Check	=	++	Bad move	=	?
Checkmate	=	#	Interesting idea	=	!?
Capture	=	x	Dubious move	=	?!
Castles kingside	=	0-0	Brilliant move	=	!!
Castles queenside	=	0-0-0	Disastrous move	=	??
See diagram 2 (etc.)	=	*(2)*	Championship	=	Ch

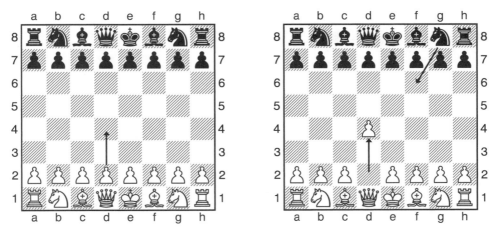

In the left-hand diagram above, White is about to play the move **1 d4**. The **1** indicates the move-number, and **d4** the destination square of the white pawn.

In the right-hand diagram, White's **1 d4** move is complete. Black is about to reply **1...♞f6** (moving his knight to the **f6-square** on his *first move*).

When a pawn promotes, the piece chosen is written immediately after the square where the pawn promotes. Thus e8♕ means that White moved his pawn to e8 and promoted to a queen.

In this book, there are some *game references*. This is a shorthand way of saying that a specific position and sequence of moves occurred in a game between two particular players. White's name is given first, followed by Black's name and the place and year where the game was played (e.g., Fischer-Spassky, Reykjavik 1972).

OVERPROTECTION

7

How to Study Strategy

Chances are you know how to play chess, and have studied some basic tactics, openings and endgames. Armed with this knowledge, you have played some games, maybe against relatives or colleagues, and you might even have ventured into the worlds of competitive or online chess. But mysteriously, you weren't able to apply all that knowledge you worked so hard to obtain. The problem is knowing what to do when you *don't* have a familiar position or pattern in front of you.

This is where strategy comes in. It is the glue that binds everything else together. It enables us to play purposefully and engineer positions where we *can* apply our knowledge. Without strategy, chess is just a game where people play purposeless moves until someone allows a tactic or blunders away a piece. Without strategy, chess would not have fascinated generations of players and it would not have been the world's most popular board game for the last few centuries.

So what *is* strategy? It is the means by which we break down chess positions into familiar elements, and build individual moves into methods and manoeuvres. So rather than simply calculating endless sequences of moves, we can look at the position schematically and determine what we should be doing.

Much of our understanding of chess strategy comes from studying the games and writings of the greatest minds in chess history. By dint of experience, they have devised rules of thumb for how to handle certain situations.

When thinking strategically, we aim to improve our position step by step. When strengthening his pawn-structure or centralizing his pieces, a grandmaster hasn't necessarily seen a specific sequence where this will benefit him directly. But he knows that these actions will almost certainly improve his game, and will lead to further opportunities to do so, and eventually lead to a tangible gain.

ACTIVE KING

Getting down to some specifics, I believe there are three main steps by which we can become skilful chess *strategists*:

1) Learn the basic strategic devices (such as development and space).

2) Recognize typical patterns where strategic themes may occur.

3) Incorporate your strategic idea with a broader plan.

Step One: Learn the Basic Strategic Devices

In this book we cover the most important strategic motifs in chess. You can find a rather broad list on the contents page, but these are some of the main ones:

Development
Centralization
Space
Pawn-Structure
Outposts
The Bishop-Pair
Open and Half-Open Files
Weak Squares
Piece Activity
Coordination
Positional Sacrifices
Pawn-Breaks
Pawn-Majority
Minority Attack

Familiarity with these strategic motifs is helpful in determining the correct plan. Some of these themes are easy to learn while others are more difficult (such as positional sacrifices). Each of these themes is explained in detail and covered as a 'Smart Strategy' in this book.

Step Two: Recognize Typical Strategic Patterns

Strong players know that certain pawn-formations make particular strategic ideas much more common. Here is a typical example to illustrate how this works (and don't worry if this goes over your head – see the note at the end of this example!):

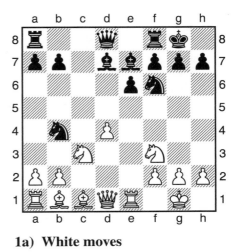

1a) White moves

Experienced players will instantly spot several strategic ideas (mini-plans) just by looking at the pawn-structure.

White has three **pawn-islands** versus Black's two (Smart Strategy 18) and should generally avoid piece exchanges, as they would make it easier for Black to exploit White's weaker pawn-structure.

White has an **isolated d4-pawn** (Smart Strategy 16), which is strong in the middlegame but weak in the endgame.

One reason the d4-pawn is strong in the middlegame is because White can **centralize** (Smart Strategy 9) a knight on the

outpost e5 (Smart Strategy 19). Black too has a very strong outpost on d5, where he wants to place the b4-knight.

In one game White played the natural move 13 ②e5 and Black answered with 13...♗c6 *(1b)*, **overprotecting** (Smart Strategy 43) the d5-square since it is the most important square in Black's position.

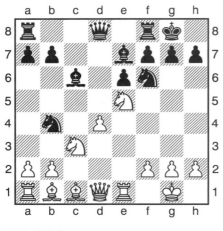

1b) White moves

White continued 14 a3, forcing the reply 14...②bd5, when the minor pieces on f6 and c6 became **superfluous** (Smart Strategy 22), creating a slight **disharmony** (Smart Strategy 39) in Black's position since they too wanted to sit on the beautiful d5-square! After 15 ♕d3, exerting pressure on the **open diagonal** b1-h7 (Smart Strategy 24), White threatened 16 ♗g5, a famous plan invented by the 4th World Champion, Alexander Alekhine (Smart Strategy 16).

Don't be troubled if you are unfamiliar with some of these concepts – after all, you haven't studied the book yet! All these themes will be explained in detail, and you will be using them in your games soon enough. My purpose here is just to show that familiarity with chess strategy will mean you are never short of ideas for how to handle a position, and will make your play far more purposeful.

Step Three: Incorporate your Strategic Idea with a Broader Plan

Beating a good chess-player requires a broad and flexible plan. The key is to combine several different strategic motifs in the one plan. Actually, as we have already seen, most strategic ideas – even simple ones – already feature more than one theme. Let's look at the very start of the game to see how this might work in a familiar context.

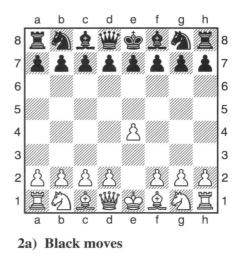

2a) Black moves

White has played 1 e4, controlling the light squares d5 and f5 in the enemy territory. The broader plan for White at this stage might be to prepare kingside castling. Another plan is to use a light-square strategy since White has already placed a pawn on a light square, where it is controlling other light squares. White would very much like to place his knights on the outposts d5 and/or f5 in the future.

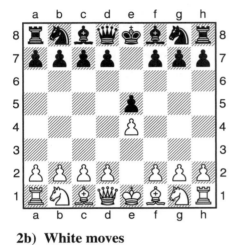

2b) White moves

Black has the same plans as White but it is White's turn to move. In this position White has a target on e5, on which he can focus his attention. He wants to put pressure on the e5-pawn and prepare a pawn-break like d4 or f4. White should adapt to the situation and change his original light-square strategy to a dark-square one. If White would like to postpone or avoid a dark-square strategy he could play a move

such as 2 ♘c3 or 2 ♗c4 (instead of 2 ♘f3) and be faithful to his initial light-square strategy. However, in chess it makes sense to modify your plans in accordance with your opponent's reactions.

Note that in Smart Strategy 1, the two diagrams above appear again, but it is not an error – we shall be discussing them from a different angle!

I hope that this brief introduction helpfully sets the scene for the strategic discussions that are to follow. Note that, as we have seen, successful planning often involves a wide range of themes, so to get the full benefit, you should read the whole book. Then you will be able to use all the themes, rather than employing just a few, which would be akin to playing a guitar that is missing a few strings. Once you have studied chess strategy for long enough, something in your mind will go *"click!"* and suddenly you will find that a vast array of chess positions make sense to you, and you will be able to sense what is required. This will be a very good feeling when it happens!

Before moving on to the 50 Smart Strategies, I should add that every position in this book, with just a few exceptions, is from a real game (including the tests at the end), both classic games as well as ones from recent events.

Control the Centre

Win the centre and control the board...

The most important squares on the board are the four in the middle. This area is called 'the centre' and should be the main focus of our attention, especially early in the game. We should aim to control the centre, and to place our pieces in the centre, since from there they radiate power in all directions. For an attack to succeed, we normally need to control at least two of these four squares – and if we can control all four of them, we can expect to dominate the board! The next step in our understanding of the centre is to think about the 'extended centre' consisting of the sixteen squares c3-c6-f6-f3 (see the first diagram below). These squares have a strong impact on the centre itself, and also tend to be excellent squares for pieces to be located.

We should note that it is generally a strategic advantage to have more pawns on the central files than the opponent. This is called a *central majority*, and it is a theme we shall encounter many times throughout this book.

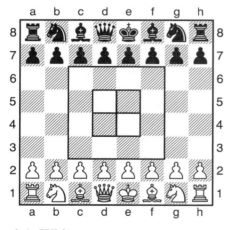

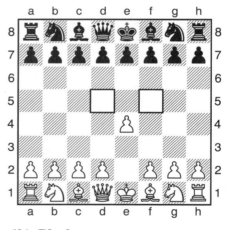

1a) White moves

Our first move of the game should control some central squares. The moves 1 e4, 1 d4, 1 c4 and 1 ♘f3 all make sense, as they control central squares in the opponent's half of the board: e5 or d5.

1b) Black moves

With 1 e4 White has controlled one square in the centre (d5) and one square in the extended centre (f5). This is an excellent move, as it also opens a path for the bishop on f1.

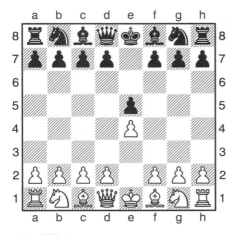

1c) White moves

Black has played the symmetrical reply 1...e5, which has all the same qualities as White's opening move. Black is fighting for control of the centre by staking a claim for the d4-square.

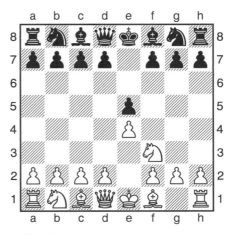

1d) Black moves

Here the knight move 2 ♘f3 has threatened the e5-pawn while contesting control of the d4-square. White is starting to prepare to castle by developing his kingside pieces.

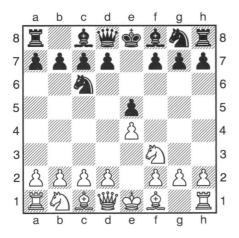

1e) White moves

Black has just defended the e5-pawn with 2...♘c6, while again fighting for control of d4 – an important central square in White's half of the board. However, Black's kingside development is slow.

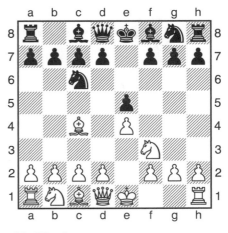

1f) Black moves

By playing 3 ♗c4, White controls the central d5-square while also eyeing the vulnerable f7-pawn. Thus White is developing while furthering his attacking plans and limiting Black's options.

Develop Your Pieces

*Get more pieces out than your opponent –
don't forget the queen's rook!*

Development means getting your pieces off their starting squares, and putting them in places where they can do something useful. The games of the American genius Paul Morphy in the 1850s showed the chess world that it is more important to play for development than for an immediate attack. Once all the pieces are developed, attacking chances will appear naturally, especially if the opponent's pieces are less well developed. These principles apply most strongly if the position is *open* – that is, if there are very few pawns in the centre. Even if the centre is not fully open, then it may be possible to blast open lines with a pawn sacrifice, as in the famous game Schulten-Morphy, New York 1857 (see diagram 2a). Remember that you haven't truly completed your development until both your rooks are in play. However, there is more to development than simply moving your pieces out: there should be a plan behind these moves. The pieces are only *well-developed* if they cooperate together.

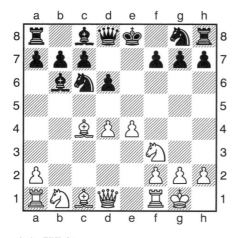

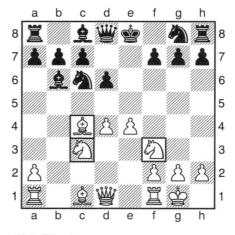

1a) White moves

Here there are some tempting aggressive possibilities like 9 d5 but calm development is best. Morphy preferred 9 ♘c3 *(1b)*, when White has three pieces out and has already castled.

1b) Black moves

Black may harass White's bishop with 9...♘a5 and after 10 ♗d3 develop rapidly with 10...♘e7 followed by 11...0-0. Generally it is better to develop knights before bishops.

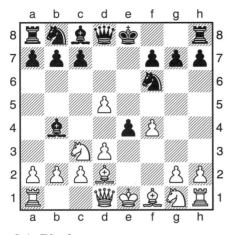

2a) Black moves

6...e3! is a typical pawn sacrifice to exploit a lead in development. After 7 ♗xe3 0-0 8 ♗d2 ♗xc3 9 bxc3 ♖e8+ 10 ♗e2 ♗g4 Black has activated most of his pieces and White must tread carefully.

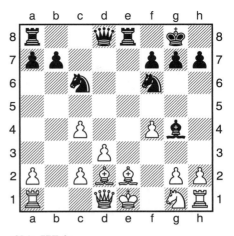

2b) White moves

This was the position a few moves later. White is two pawns up but behind in development and his king is exposed on the e-file. 13...♘d4 is coming next, cranking up the pressure to unbearable levels.

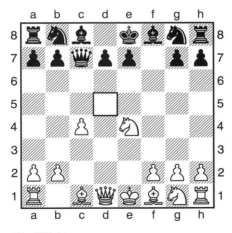

3) White moves

Often development is more important than material. A logical move is 7 ♘e2!, planning ♘2c3-d5. White should not be put off by 7...♕xc4? 8 ♘2c3, since he then has a large lead in development.

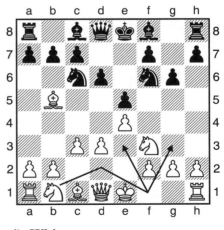

4) White moves

In closed positions, getting pieces to their best squares may take priority over pure speed of development. After 6 ♘bd2 ♗g7 7 ♘f1 0-0 8 ♘e3, White's knight is well centralized, controlling the d5-square.

The strongest central formation

One of White's basic strategic aims is to establish pawns on d4 and e4. This is a goal he might try to achieve in the first few moves, or else to do so later in the middlegame, after more preparation. This set-up is called the Classical Centre. Why is it considered strong? These pawns control the four squares c5, d5, e5 and f5, and unless Black can break White's grip, it will be very hard for him to establish his pieces on good squares, or to challenge White's grip on the position.

This is probably the strongest central formation if it can be maintained and exploited. But that is a big 'if', since if Black has been developing his pieces while White has been moving his pawns, he should be able to respond with piece-play or a pawn-break (see diagram 2). However, if Black has squandered his chances, the pawns can become an unstoppable steamroller (see diagram 1).

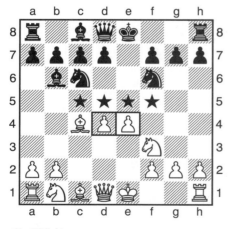

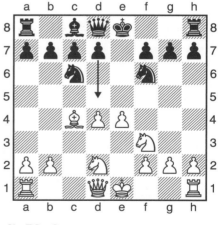

1) White moves

Black has played the Giuoco Piano carelessly. Now 7 d5! ♘e7 8 e5! drives the black knights to rotten squares while seizing space and creating the conditions for a successful attack.

2) Black moves

Another position from the same opening, but here Black can break up the centre with 8...d5!. After 9 exd5 ♘xd5 White has just one pawn in the centre, and Black can develop his pieces in comfort.

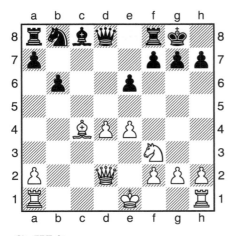

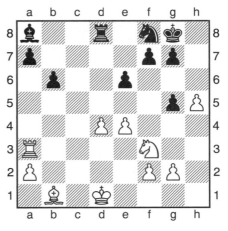

3) White moves

If the classical centre is also a *majority*, then it may be used to create a central *passed pawn*. Here White can play 12 d5 ♗a6 13 ♗xa6 ♘xa6 14 d6, with an influential passed pawn on d6.

4) Black moves

If fighting against a classical centre, one idea is to swap some pieces. Breaking up the centre is even better: here Black plays 26...g4 27 ♘d2 ♖xd4 28 ♖xa7 ♗c6, a profitable exchange of pawns.

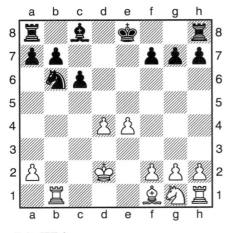

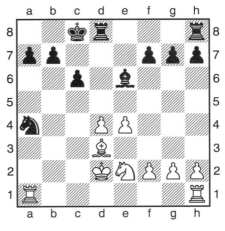

5a) White moves

After an exchange of queens, a pawn-centre can be used as shelter for the king, to help activate it for the endgame. Note how safe the king is after 15 ♗d3 ♗e6 16 a4 0-0-0 17 ♘e2 ♘xa4 18 ♖a1 *(5b)*.

5b) Black moves

After 18...♘b2 19 ♖xa7 ♔b8 20 ♖ha1 ♗c4 21 ♗xc4 ♘xc4+ 22 ♔d3 White's king is well centralized behind the central pawns. He can look forward to the endgame with confidence.

The Little Centre

Freedom for the pieces to manoeuvre

The structure arises after an exchange of one pair of pawns in the centre leaves only one player with a pawn on a central square. The first two diagrams below show two typical cases. The fact that an exchange of pawns (...exd4 or ...dxe4) has taken place means that this is not a closed position, but nor is it fully open. You could call it a half-open (or half-closed) pawn-formation. Speed of development will be important, but so will making sure the pieces achieve good footholds.

   The little centre stakes out an advantage in territory for its possessor. In such a structure the general rule is to avoid piece exchanges because the defender has less space to manoeuvre his pieces. The defender can either seek a freeing pawn-break (which could lead to a fully open centre) or else manoeuvre and seek beneficial exchanges.

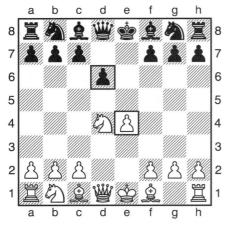

1a) Black moves

   This arises after 1 e4 e5 2 ♘f3 d6 3 d4 exd4 4 ♘xd4. White's knights have potential strong squares on f5 and d5 but Black's *outposts* are further back in his position on c5 and e5.

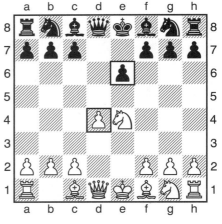

1b) Black moves

   This similar-looking position is the result of 1 e4 e6 2 d4 d5 3 ♘c3 dxe4 4 ♘xe4. White has occupied four ranks, and Black three, while the fifth rank is a 'no-man's land', free from occupation.

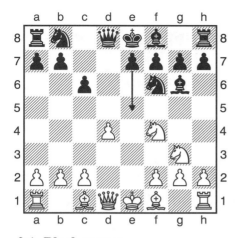

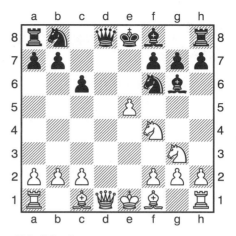

2a) Black moves

The defender may not have to adopt a submissive role. Sometimes he can destroy the little centre with a move like 7...e5!. White is obliged to agree to the exchange with 8 dxe5 *(2b)*.

2b) Black moves

After 8...♕xd1+ 9 ♔xd1 ♘g4 Black wins back the pawn, while after 8...♕a5+ 9 c3 ♕xe5+ 10 ♕e2 ♘bd7 the little centre has been transformed into an open centre and Black has no real problems.

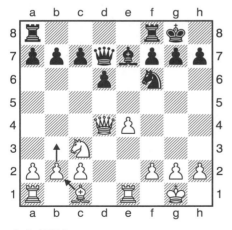

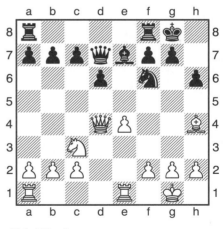

3a) White moves

When you have a space advantage it is important to keep plenty of pieces on the board. 11 b3 followed by 12 ♗b2 puts pressure on the a1-h8 diagonal and makes it hard for Black to exchange bishops.

3b) Black moves

Black frees his game with 12...♘g4, practically forcing the exchange 13 ♗xe7 ♕xe7. The aggressive 14 ♘d5 is answered by 14...♕e5, securing the exchange of queens.

Other Types of Pawn-Centre

Get to know other central structures

There are many different central pawn-configurations, and here we shall take a quick look at three of the more noteworthy ones, by which White can stake out a space advantage. In all these cases it is important to know the typical ideas both as an attacker and as a defender. The first is the Maroczy Bind (diagrams 1 and 2), where White's pawns on c4 and e4 exert a grip on the position. Although Black has more pawns on the central files, it is hard for him to advance them.

Our two remaining structures feature one or two open files, but White's pawns are further advanced, claiming a space advantage in more direct fashion.

As a general rule in all these structures, the defender should aim to exchange pieces, as he has less space. Another strategy is to transform the pawn-centre into one that gives his pieces more freedom. The attacker prefers to keep the central structure intact while avoiding piece exchanges. The main task is then to create weaknesses in the enemy position.

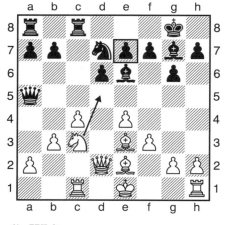

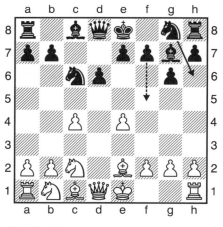

1) White moves

This pawn-structure is called the Maroczy Bind. 14 ♘d5! puts pressure on the weak e7-pawn. After 14...♕xd2+ 15 ♔xd2 ♗xd5 16 cxd5 White has more space and the *bishop-pair* (see Smart Strategy 28).

2) Black moves

One way for Black to fight back is to attack the e4-pawn with 7...♘h6 8 0-0 f5. White cannot defend his central pawn in any convenient way, and so cannot maintain the status quo. Black has broken the 'bind' and a sharp fight lies ahead.

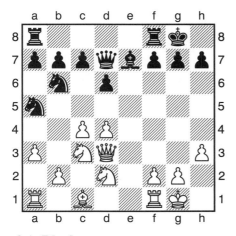

3a) Black moves

13...d5 stops White playing d5, but after 14 c5 ♘bc4 15 ♘f3 White has a space advantage on the queenside and avoids exchanges. Black may prefer a simplifying approach with 13...♕e6 and 14...♕g6.

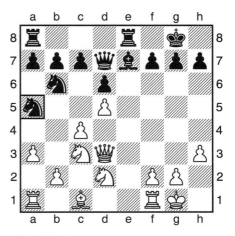

3b) Black moves

Here Black has unsuspectingly played 13...♖fe8?, and White has claimed an advantage in space with 14 d5!, locking out the a5-knight from the game while threatening b4.

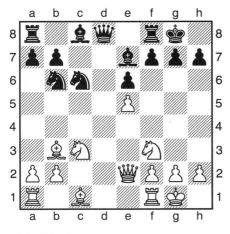

4a) Black moves

White's pawn on e5 allows him to bring pieces over to attack the black king and makes it hard for defending pieces to come to his aid. The e4-square can be used for a knight or a queen.

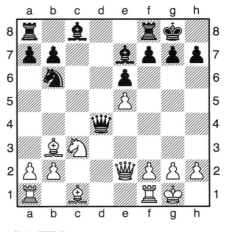

4b) White moves

Here Black has opted for a trade of knights with 12...♘d4? 13 ♘xd4 ♕xd4. After 14 ♖d1 ♕h4, the 'rook-lift' 15 ♖d3, threatening 16 ♖h3, gives White excellent attacking chances.

SMART STRATEGY 6

Tension in the Centre

Force the opponent to release the tension

Pawn 'tension' means a situation where a black pawn and a white pawn are one square diagonally apart, and so either of them could capture the other one. An example is the pawns on d5 and e4 in our first diagram below. Whether to maintain the tension (by leaving the pawns as they are) or to release it (by taking or by advancing our pawn) is often a crucial strategic decision. It may also be possible to increase the tension even further. There will normally be at least one decision like this in the opening, and several more in the middlegame.

The general rule is that *releasing the tension is a concession*. The point is that while the tension exists, the opponent must be ready for several possibilities, and once it is released, it is easier to plan a strategy. That said, each situation should be assessed on its own merits, and if you see a way to resolve tension in your favour, then it makes sense to do so.

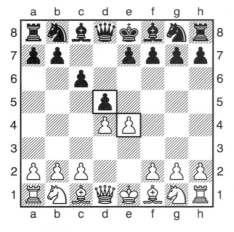

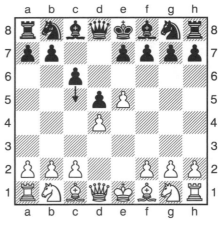

1a) White moves

In some openings, tension arises as early as the second move. Black's last move, 2...d5, creates tension and White must react accordingly. White can release the tension with 3 exd5 or 3 e5 *(1b)*.

1b) Black moves

White has gained space but granted Black the possibility of ...♗f5. Black can create tension again with 3...c5, when White can choose 4 dxc5 (release), 4 c3 (maintain) or 4 c4, increasing the tension.

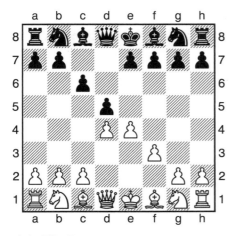

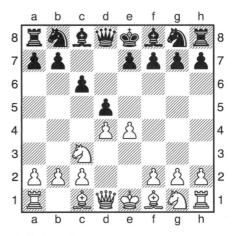

1c) Black moves

White has played 3 f3, keeping the tension, and seeking a classical centre after 3...dxe4 4 fxe4. Black can crank up the tension to the maximum by 3...e5!?, with complex gambit play after 4 dxe5 ♝c5.

1d) Black moves

White has chosen 3 ♘c3, which is the most natural way to maintain the tension. It is hard for Black to find a better move than 3...dxe4, when 4 ♘xe4 gives us a 'little centre' – see Smart Strategy 4.

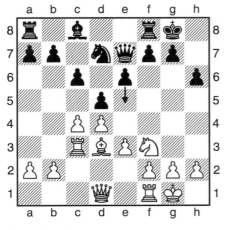

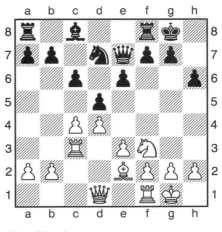

2a) Black moves

Black needs to find a way to develop his bishop, and plays 12...e5!. Black threatens ...e4 so White must release the tension: 13 dxe5 dxc4! 14 ♝xc4 ♘xe5 15 ♘xe5 ♛xe5 and the c8-bishop is free.

2b) Black moves

When the bishop is on e2, creating tension with 12...e5? does not work because 13 dxe5 dxc4 14 ♛d6! leaves White well-placed. So Black plays 12...dxc4! 13 ♝xc4 b6 followed by ...♝b7 and ...c5.

Extend your arsenal by playing in a hypermodern way

So far, we have been looking mainly at plans to *occupy* the centre in the opening. But this is not the only viable option. It is also possible to control the centre with pieces from a distance, and thus prevent the opponent from occupying it. Or even to let the opponent occupy the centre, and then show that *occupation is not the same as control*, and attack this centre with pieces and pawns.

The idea of controlling the centre from a distance – the *hypermodern* method – was a hot topic of debate in the 1920s. It was opposed by the *classical* school, which favoured occupation. In modern chess, both approaches are used, as either can prove more effective in any given position: the pragmatic modern method is to play whatever works.

To give some examples, with 1 e4 White is using a classical approach, while after 1 ♘f3, perhaps followed by 2 b3 and 3 ♗b2, we have a hypermodern opening.

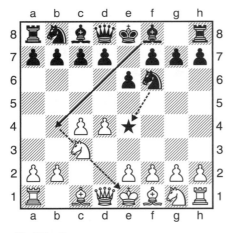

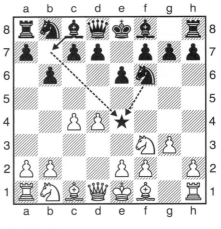

1) Black moves

Now 3...♗b4 is the Nimzo-Indian Defence. The idea is to control the e4-square thanks to the pin on the white knight. In this way Black keeps a more flexible position than he would with the more 'classical' 3...d5.

2) Black moves

This is the Queen's Indian Defence. Here too Black is controlling the e4-square with his pieces. 4...♗b7 is the obvious move, but there is also the subtle 4...♗a6, inconveniencing White by attacking the c4-pawn, before later playing ...♗b7.

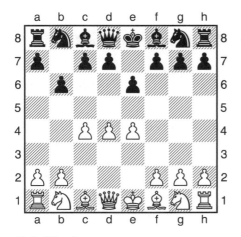

3a) Black moves

Here we see an even more extreme example of hypermodern chess: White has been allowed to occupy the whole centre. Black strikes back with 3...♗b7 4 ♘c3 ♗b4 5 ♗d3 f5 *(3b)*.

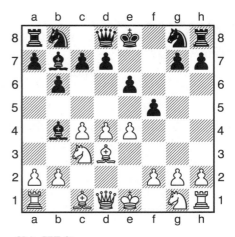

3b) White moves

Black is throwing all his resources into the assault on White's pawn-centre. Great care is needed by both sides as tricky tactics and surprising pawn sacrifices abound in such a wild position.

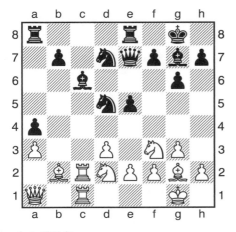

4a) White moves

This is a typical middlegame resulting from a hypermodern opening. White has three of his pieces trained on the e5-pawn. Now 19 e4! ♘c7 20 d4! *(4b)* brings the central pawns into the assault.

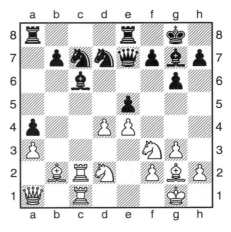

4b) Black moves

After 20...exd4 21 ♘xd4 it is White who is occupying the centre rather than Black. In hypermodern chess, occupation of the centre is merely *delayed* until true control can be maintained, not avoided forever.

Neutralization of the Centre

Make your opponent's centre less impressive

We have already seen a few ideas for fighting against the opponent's pawn-centre, but it is often preferable to prevent him from creating one in the first place. A standard method is to make one exchange of pawns in the centre and then create tension by attacking the centre with another pawn (it is not as complicated as it sounds – see the first diagram below for a very clear example). If the opponent releases the tension, then there may not be much left of his pawn-centre. But if he maintains the tension, then he must, on each turn, take into account the possibility of an exchange of pawns. It may also be effective to attack our opponent's remaining central pawn with our pieces. The point is to force him to guard his precious central foothold, and so prevent further expansion. A simple example occurs after 1 d4 d5 2 c4 dxc4 3 e3 c5. Although White has two pawns vs one on the central files, it will be hard for him to advance his e-pawn to e4 without allowing an exchange of his d4-pawn.

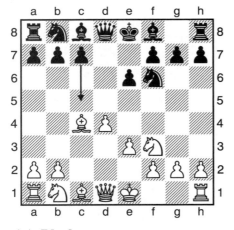

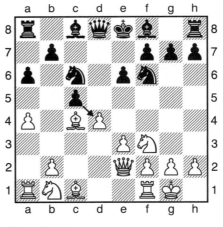

1a) Black moves

Black has already exchanged his d-pawn for White's c-pawn. Now he plays 5...c5. Black plans to exchange pawns on d4 when the moment is right. After 6 0-0 a6 7 a4 ♘c6 8 ♕e2 we have diagram 1b.

1b) Black moves

By exchanging with 8...cxd4, Black equalizes the pawn-count on the central files. After 9 ♖d1 ♗e7 White's best option is 10 exd4, creating an *isolated queen's pawn* (see Smart Strategy 16).

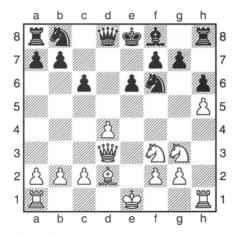

2a) Black moves

Even though White has no central majority here, it makes sense to attack the d4-pawn with 11...c5. Otherwise c4 and d5 might become a strong plan for White. 12 0-0-0 ♘c6 13 ♗c3 ♕d5 *(2b)* may follow.

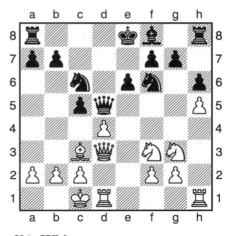

2b) White moves

White releases the tension by 14 dxc5 because of Black's ideas of ...♕xa2 and ...c4. The sequence of exchanges with 14...♕xd3 15 ♖xd3 ♗xc5 16 ♗xf6 gxf6 17 ♘e4 ♗e7 leaves the position balanced.

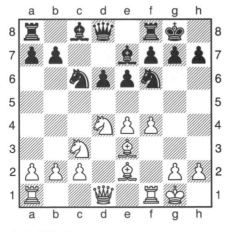

3a) Black moves

This is the Modern Scheveningen, a line of the Sicilian Defence. With 9...e5 Black wants to trade off the e5-pawn for the white f-pawn. White may reply 10 ♘b3 exf4 11 ♗xf4 ♗e6 12 ♔h1 *(3b)*.

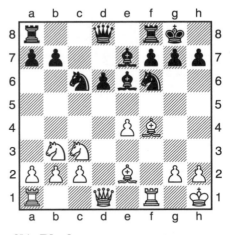

3b) Black moves

12...d5 challenges White's grip on the centre. White plays either 13 exd5 ♘xd5 with an open centre or 13 e5 ♘e4 with chances for both sides since they both have a strong pawn in the centre.

Piece Centralization

The soundest plan in chess history

We have already talked a lot about putting, or not putting, pawns in the centre. But the overall aim of controlling the centre, however it is accomplished, is to establish *pieces* in the centre. A centralized piece radiates power in all directions and controls a number of important squares, helping with our own plans and hindering the opponent's ideas.

In the early part of the game, once we have a foothold in the centre and have developed most of our pieces, we may have a good opportunity to place a knight on a central square, supported by a pawn. The second world champion, Emanuel Lasker, even described this as "the soundest plan in chess history". Quite a recommendation! As the knight is a short-range piece, it benefits even more from a central location than a bishop, rook or queen, which can all prove effective from afar.

One point to bear in mind is that a piece doesn't control the square it is on, so occupying a central square might not be a great idea if there is a full-scale battle in progress for control of the square in question.

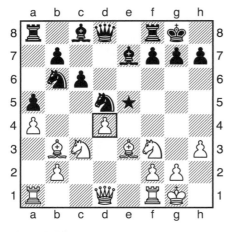

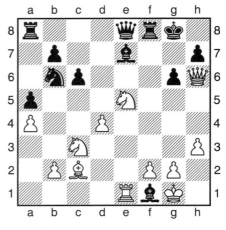

1a) White moves

This is one of the de la Bourdonnais-McDonnell games in 1834. 13 ♘e5 places the knight in enemy territory, increases the pressure on f7 and allows the white queen into the attack.

1b) White moves

The position some moves later. The sacrifice 22 ♗xg6! works thanks to the centralized knight. After 22...hxg6 23 ♘xg6 ♘c8 24 ♕h8+ ♔f7 25 ♕h7+ ♔f6 26 ♘f4! the knight weaves a mating-net.

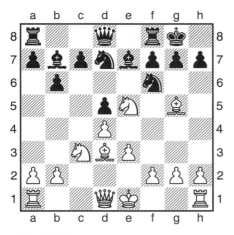

2a) White moves

10 f4 secures the knight in the centre and lays the groundwork for a kingside attack. Now 10...c5 11 0-0 c4?! 12 ♗c2 a6? *(2b)* (12...h6! 13 ♗h4 ♘e8 is safer) allows White a very strong attack.

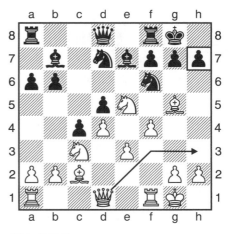

2b) White moves

13 ♕f3 (the queen controls the e4-square and threatens 14 ♘xc4, exploiting a pin) 13...b5 14 ♕h3 (the real plan) 14...g6 15 f5! broke open more lines of attack in Pillsbury-Marco, Paris 1900.

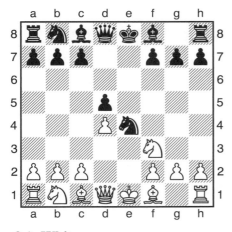

3a) White moves

This is from an opening called the Petroff Defence. White's plan is based on attacking the e4-knight; e.g., 6 ♗d3 ♘c6 7 0-0 ♗e7 8 c4 *(3b)*, undermining the pawn that supports the knight.

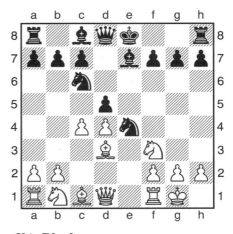

3b) Black moves

One way for Black to keep a solid position is now 8...♘f6, but note that he has then lost time with this knight. Here the knight had occupied a central square before control had been established.

Space Advantage

Avoid piece exchanges when in possession of space

We have already touched upon the subject of a space advantage when we discussed the little centre in Smart Strategy 4. Normally having more space than the opponent is to our advantage, as it means his pieces tend to get in each other's way. But there are positions where it offers little benefit or may even be a problem. Everything depends on how much play our opponent has. Pawn-breaks (see Smart Strategy 42) are one way to free a cramped position, and there are cases where he can manoeuvre his pieces without any problems within his apparently confined camp. If we cannot even control 'our' space, then the enemy pieces might break into the squares behind our pawns and start wreaking havoc.

When we have the space advantage we normally try to avoid piece exchanges whenever possible. This makes it harder for our opponent to find the necessary room for his pieces. When that job is done, we can use our advantage in space to initiate some kind of attack on one of the flanks.

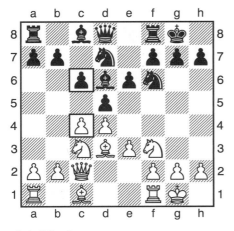

1a) Black moves

Space gives us options. The c4-pawn puts pressure on the centre while the c6-pawn just defends. White could play cxd5 or c5, gaining queenside space. Black's only option with the c6-pawn is ...c5.

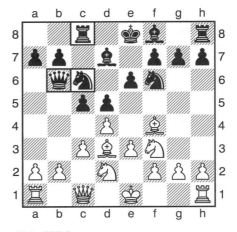

1b) White moves

Here Black enjoys the type of space advantage that White normally has. Black has slightly more freedom for his pieces. Note the active queen, rook, knight and pawn on the queenside.

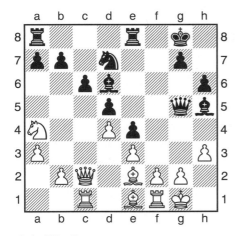

2a) Black moves

Black wisely avoided the exchange on e2 and instead used the strong e4-pawn to attack the king with the clever 19...♗f3!. After 20 ♗xf3 exf3 21 g3 ♕h5 22 ♔h2 *(2b)* Black has a winning attack.

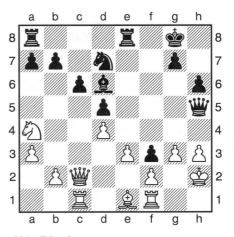

2b) Black moves

Black's pawn has been transferred from the centre to the kingside and cut White's position in two parts with the strong wedge on f3. Sometimes such a pawn has the same value as a piece.

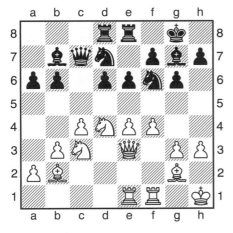

3a) White moves

White has more space and looks ready for a kingside attack, but lacks a real plan to improve his position. After the seemingly natural 18 g4?! ♘c5 *(3b)* Black's well-organized forces take over the game.

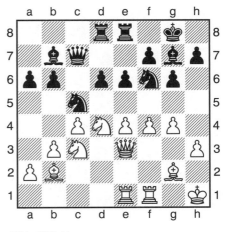

3b) White moves

Black is ready to make the strong ...e5 pawn-break, and 19 g5? is answered by 19...♘h5, when all Black's pieces will be liberated by ...e5. White's pawn advances have left irreparable weaknesses.

SMART STRATEGY 11 — United Pawns

Advance the pawns in a phalanx

Pawns are strong and flexible when they stand side-by-side. Each one protects the square in front of its neighbour. If one of the pawns advances, it will be protected by the other pawn. In the initial position, all the pawns are united, but naturally we must advance some of them to allow the pieces to develop. The ideal then is to advance the pawns in a phalanx (side-by-side), supported by the pieces. Of course our opponent will do his best to destroy our dreams of a strong phalanx, sweeping everything from their path. When our phalanx comes under attack, our back-up plan may be to construct a chain of pawns, which brings us to the next theme – see Smart Strategy 12.

We have already touched on centralized and united pawns on d4 and e4 in Smart Strategy 3 when we discussed the classical centre. In 2a-2c we examine ways to attack and maintain this pawn duo, while our final two diagrams are from a game Keres-Petrosian in the 1959 Candidates tournament. Petrosian (World Champion 1963-9) advances his pawns flexibly and in unison to drive back the enemy pieces and gain the initiative.

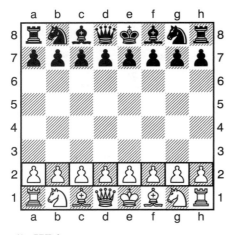

1) White moves

In the initial position all white and black pawns are united and weakness-free. The challenge is develop the pieces while keeping a sound structure.

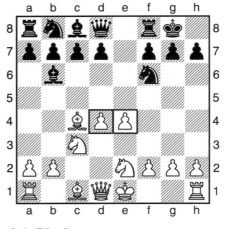

2a) Black moves

White has a two-abreast pawn-centre. However, Black can break them up with 7...♘xe4!, based on the pawn fork 8 ♘xe4 d5. Tactics often serve strategic purposes.

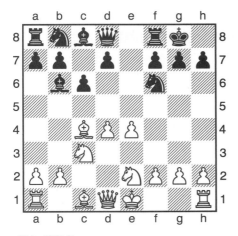

2b) White moves

Black is preparing ...d5. White can reply 8 ♗d3, so that he can keep his pawns united. Then 8...d5 *(2c)* gains a foothold in the centre and challenges White to resolve the central tension.

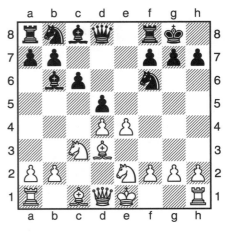

2c) White moves

White has a classic choice: defend, exchange or advance. 9 exd5 cxd5 gives no advantage in the centre, while 9 f3?! dxe4 10 fxe4 ♗xd4 loses a pawn. 9 e5 gains time and a space advantage.

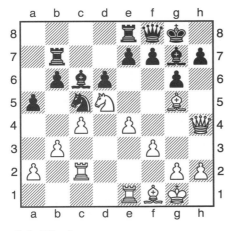

3a) Black moves

Black looks passive, but watch how he uses his pawns: with 27...f6 he releases the pressure on the e7-pawn and drives back the bishop. After 28 ♗e3 e6 29 ♘c3 *(3b)* he has also driven back the knight.

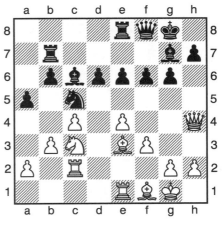

3b) Black moves

Black's pawns on d6-g6 look odd, but there are no real weaknesses. Will Black go for ...d5, ...e5, ...f5 or ...g5? White must be ready for many plans. After 29...♖d7 30 ♗d4 f5! Black later won.

The Pawn-Chain

When you cannot hold the phalanx, create a pawn-chain!

A pawn-chain is a diagonal line of pawns. This way, they defend one another, with the exception of the pawn at the back – the *base* pawn. A pawn-chain is often blocked, at least in part, by the opponent's own pawn-chain on the opposite-coloured squares. This makes both pawn-chains unable to move, and thus a *static* feature of the position. Pawn-chains are a major element of chess strategy, as they stake out space and have a huge impact on the bishops, by either complementing or obstructing each bishop. When the front pawn of the chain is placed on its fifth rank, it can provide the basis for an attack by controlling key squares and keeping defensive forces at bay.

Therefore we may wish to break up an enemy pawn-chain. A dramatic way is with a piece sacrifice, but pure pawn-play can also do the trick. Attacking the base of the chain weakens the support of the other pawns, but takes time. Attacking and exchanging the pawn at the front of the chain is strategically double-edged, but may be a good way to neutralize threats.

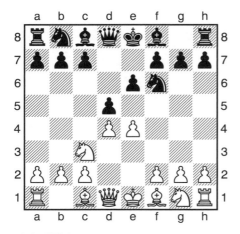

1a) White moves

White's two-abreast pawn-centre is under attack. One way to solve this problem is to advance with 4 e5 ♘fd7 5 f4 *(1b)*, setting up a pawn-chain.

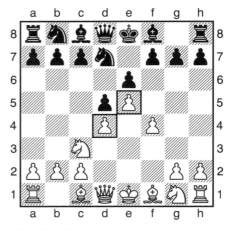

1b) Black moves

After 5...c5 (attacking the base), one possibility is 6 ♘f3 ♘c6 7 ♘e2 ♛b6 8 c3, securely supporting the chain. Black can then attack the front pawn with 8...f6.

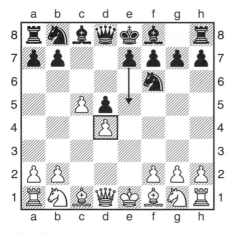

2) Black moves

It is not a good idea to set up a chain on the flank early in the game before developing many pieces. Black shatters the fragile base with 5...e5! 6 dxe5 ♘e4 7 b4? a5! and the whole chain collapses.

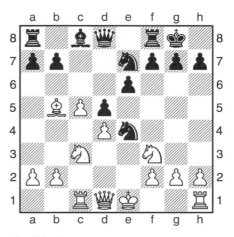

3) Black moves

White has made better preparations for setting up his chain, but 11...b6! attacks its front to good effect. 12 b4?! bxc5 13 dxc5 allows Black a strong pawn-centre, while 12 c6 gives Black the d6-square.

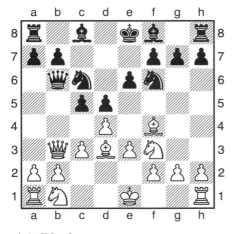

4a) Black moves

7...c4 releases the pressure on the d4-pawn, but Black now plans to attack the c3-pawn. White must trade queens by 8 ♕xb6 axb6 9 ♗e2 *(4b)*, giving Black a *half-open* a-file (Smart Strategy 29).

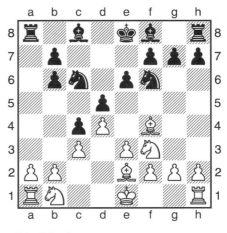

4b) Black moves

9...b5 initiates a classic plan: an attack on the fixed pawn on c3 with ...b4 and ...bxc3. He will then play ...b5 and ...b4 again, attacking the new base of the chain on c3, with strong queenside play.

The Passed Pawn

The pawn has a lust to expand

A passed pawn is one that has no enemy pawns in front of it, on its own file or the neighbouring ones. Only the enemy pieces lie between this pawn and promotion. A passed pawn is therefore a valuable asset, and sometimes enough to win the game on its own. Both players need to be highly alert to ways that the pawn might advance, as it could be worth a major material sacrifice to open the way for the pawn. Aron Nimzowitsch, one of the great writers on chess strategy, noted that a passed pawn has a "lust to expand". Promotion is not the only plan; its advance can destroy the coordination of the enemy forces, open lines of attack and create a wedge in the opponent's position. *Blockading* a passed pawn is therefore a very high priority for the defender, preferably by firmly placing a knight on the square in front of the pawn.

In the endgame, a passed pawn that is far away from the kings is called an *outside* passed pawn. It is valuable because it can tie up the defender's pieces while the attacker wins on the other side of the board.

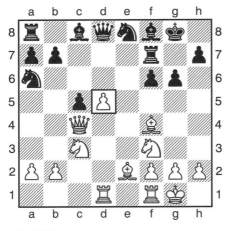

1) White moves

The passed pawn on d5 disorganizes the enemy position with 15 d6! and opens up a pin on the black rook. The pawn is poisoned: 15...♞xd6? 16 ♗xd6 ♗xd6 17 ♞b5.

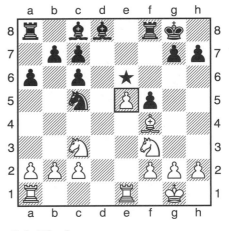

2a) Black moves

White's passed pawn brings him little joy here. 13...♞e6 is an excellent blockade that White will find very difficult to lift. After 14 ♗d2 Black plays 14...g5 (*2b*).

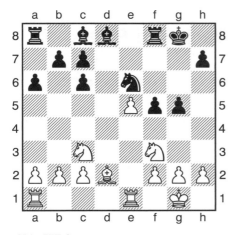

2b) White moves

Black sets his kingside pawns in motion, with excellent play. His pieces are well placed and White has very little activity. If 15 ♘e2 intending ♘ed4, then 15...c5 stamps out this idea.

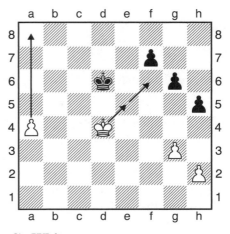

3) White moves

After the outside passed a-pawn entices the black king to the queenside, White will attack the abandoned kingside: 42 a5 f6 (or 42...♔c6 43 ♔e5) 43 a6 ♔c6 44 a7 ♔b7 45 ♔d5 h4 46 ♔e6 with a win.

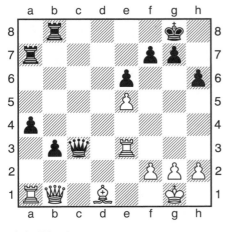

4a) Black moves

27...♕xa1! sacrifices the queen to mobilize the a- and b-pawns. 28 ♕xa1 b2 29 ♕b1 ♖c7 30 ♖e1 ♖c1 31 ♗c2 ♖xb1 32 ♗xb1 ♖c8 33 ♔f1 ♖c1 34 ♗a2 ♖a1 35 ♗b1 ♖xb1 36 ♖xb1 (4b).

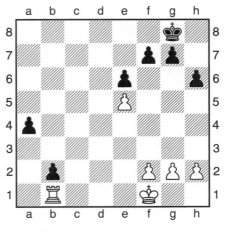

4a) Black moves

Black is a rook down, but he wins due to the power of his passed pawns: 36...a3 37 ♔e2 a2 38 ♖xb2 a1♕. The general rule is that two connected passed pawns on their sixth rank overpower a rook.

The Backward Pawn

The square in front of the pawn is the true weakness

A backward pawn is one that can't be supported by either neighbouring pawn because they have advanced ahead of it. If the square in front of the backward pawn is firmly under enemy control, then the pawn may become a target for the enemy pieces, as it is fixed in place and needs piece support. It is often not the pawn itself, but the square in front of the pawn that is the main problem. This square can be an excellent *outpost* for an enemy piece, especially a knight.

In modern chess, there has been a reassessment of backward pawns, which are no longer as feared as was once the case. Modern players are often willing to accept a backward pawn, enemy outpost and all, in return for making gains of other types. This requires a profound understanding of chess dynamics, but generally the pawn needs to be easily defended, and a good deal of piece activity needs to be generated, or else enemy pieces forced to poor locations. Some major lines of the Sicilian Defence, the most popular opening of all, are based on these nuances.

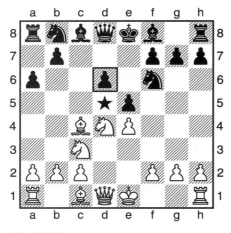

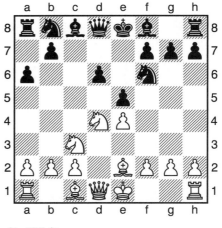

1) White moves

Black's d6-pawn is defended by the f8-bishop but the d5-square is under White's control. The strongest continuation is 7 ♘f5! planning either 8 ♗g5 or 8 ♘e3 with permanent control of d5.

2) White moves

This looks similar, but there is a big difference: White cannot dominate d5 here. After 7 ♘b3 ♗e7 and ...♗e6 Black has sufficient control of the d5-square, while 7 ♘f5?! is strongly met by 7...d5!.

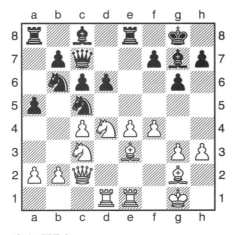

3a) White moves

The backward d6-pawn in the King's Indian Defence doesn't look highly vulnerable, but can prove a tactical weakness: 18 ♘db5! cxb5 19 ♘xb5 ♕e7 20 ♘xd6 and White wins material.

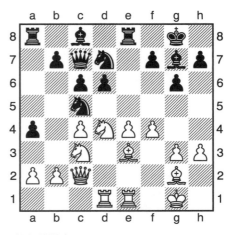

3b) White moves

In this slightly changed situation, the sacrifice is playable but now it garners only three pawns. 18 ♘db5! cxb5 19 ♘xb5 ♕a5 20 ♘xd6 followed by 21 e5 offers White some advantage.

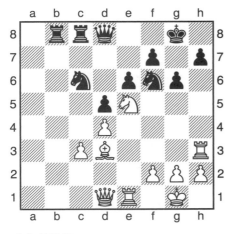

4a) White moves

In this position, from one of Kasparov's early games, White's backward c3-pawn is somewhat weak. However, the game is about equal because White has counterchances on the kingside to compensate.

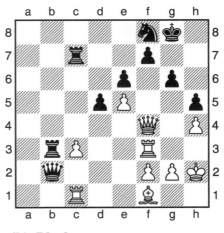

4b) Black moves

Some moves later, Kasparov exploited the concrete peculiarities of the position with 31...d4!, winning the backward pawn since 32 c4? fails to 32...♖xf3 33 gxf3 (33 ♕xf3? ♕xc1) 33...♕xf2+.

Doubled Pawns

Doubled pawns mean open lines for the rooks!

As a consequence of the pawn's diagonal capturing move, two pawns can end up on the same file. These are called doubled pawns. They are not necessarily a weakness – indeed in some respects they can be quite strong – but they can lead to problems of various types. They can be hard to advance, and so if they are attacked, they may not be able to escape. The fact that there are two pawns on one file means that there is also a file with no pawns, and this may be an invasion route for the enemy pieces, and there may be some squares left weak by the pawn's absence. On the other hand, this open file may be valuable for one of our own rooks.

In the middlegame, doubled pawns that control central squares can be a strategic plus – thus the general rule 'capture towards the centre', though there are exceptions when speed of development is the priority. In the endgame, doubled pawns can be a particular problem, as they may result in a *crippled majority* – that is, one that cannot produce a passed pawn.

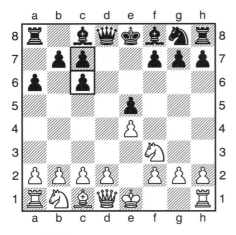

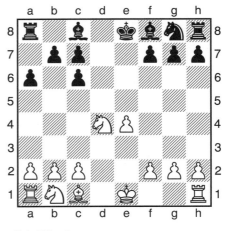

1a) White moves

Black has doubled pawns, but his development is fast, and he has bishop vs knight – a strategic plus more often than not. 5 d4 exd4 6 ♕xd4 ♕xd4 7 ♘xd4 (*1b*) leads to a queenless middlegame.

1b) Black moves

If all the pieces were traded off, the pawn ending would be lost for Black. That's because White can create a passed pawn on the kingside, whereas Black cannot do the same on the queenside.

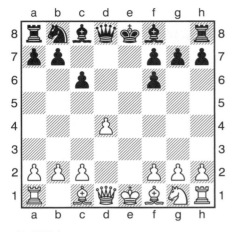

2) White moves

Black has rapid development but a crippled kingside majority. White's best plan is to attack on the kingside and exploit the weak f5-square, though he will be happy to simplify into an endgame.

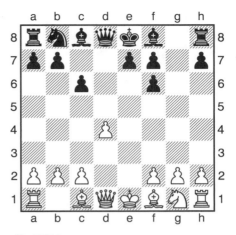

3) White moves

A similar position, but totally different strategies! Black has captured toward the centre and seeks play on the g-file. White's plan of g3 and ♗g2 neutralizes that idea and prepares a queenside attack.

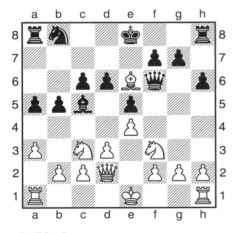

4) Black moves

Don't avoid doubled pawns 'on principle'! The best move here is 11...fxe6!, a voluntary doubling. Black strengthens his control of d5 and f5 and gives his rook a very useful *half-open* f-file.

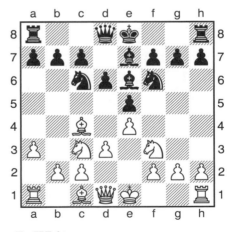

5) White moves

Think before doubling enemy pawns. 7 ♗xe6 fxe6 gives Black good central control, but after 7 ♘g5!? ♗xc4 8 dxc4 the c4-pawn gives White a strong grip on the d5-square as well as a half-open d-file.

The Isolated Pawn

Either a weakness or a strength – or both!

An isolated pawn is one that has no friendly pawns on neighbouring files. For instance, a d-pawn when the c- and e-pawns have been exchanged off. An isolated pawn is generally a weakness since it cannot be defended by another pawn. So if it is attacked, it needs to be defended by a piece, and pieces should normally be put to better use than defending stray pawns. However, with an isolated pawn on one of the centre squares (e.g. d4), matters are not so clear-cut. This pawn stakes out a space advantage and controls some important squares; it is also easy to defend without misplacing any pieces. This creates an interesting and complex strategic imbalance. An isolated pawn becomes weaker as more pieces are exchanged, because it is easier to attack while the dynamic possibilities are reduced. It is not just the pawn itself that is weak, but also the square in front of it, which is an excellent and secure square for an enemy piece. Blockading the isolated pawn fixes it as a target and prevents its advance. This is important because a sudden advance by the pawn is a common tactical ploy to unleash the pent-up energy of the pieces behind it.

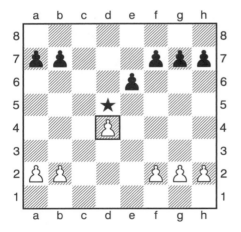

1) The isolated queen's pawn (IQP)

The d4-pawn is isolated. The d5-square is a secure post for a black piece. White has many open lines and a very useful square on e5 for a knight.

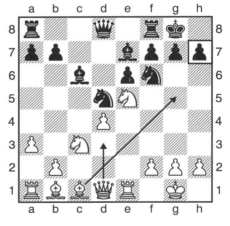

2) White moves

Both sides have occupied their strong-points in this pawn-structure. Now ♕d3 followed by ♗g5 provokes a weakness like ...g6, creating *holes* on f6 and h6.

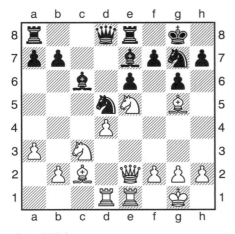

3a) White moves

Black wants to exchange pieces, which White avoids with 23 ♗c1. We see this again after 23...♘f5 24 ♘e4 ♘d6 25 ♘c5 (*3b*): White keeps the pieces on and seeks attacking chances in the middlegame.

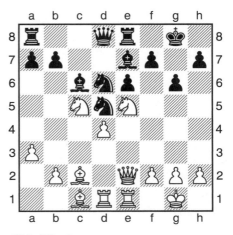

3b) Black moves

White has established knights on both outposts (c5 and e5). Black has also fortified his knight on the key square in front of the isolated pawn. A tough fight lies ahead; both sides have chances.

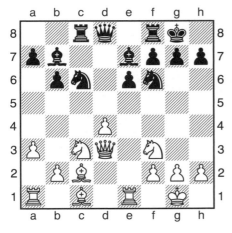

4) White moves

14 d5! is a strong and typical thrust by the IQP. Black has enormous problems because 14...exd5? loses to 15 ♗g5 (threatening ♗xf6) 15...g6 16 ♖xe7! ♕xe7 17 ♘xd5 – a sequence to remember.

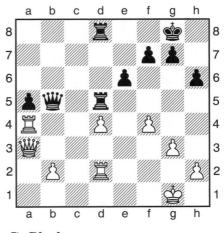

5) Black moves

The other side of the coin: 35...e5! exploits the weakness of the IQP in a simplified position. 36 fxe5 ♖xe5 37 ♕a1 ♕e8! 38 dxe5 ♖xd2 39 ♖xa5 ♕c6 gives Black a decisive attack on the white king.

The Isolated Pawn Couple and Hanging Pawns

The family tree

These are both structures that can arise from an isolated queen's pawn (IQP) following a standard change in the structure, though they can also come about by other means. In both cases, one side (let's say White) has c- and d-pawns but no b- or e-pawns. Meanwhile Black has no pawns on the c- and d-files. Thus White has an 'isolated' pair of pawns. When both pawns are on their fourth rank, they have a special name: *hanging pawns*. In that case they don't protect each other, but they pose more of a threat to the opponent, as either pawn might advance aggressively at any moment. Given their potent attacking force, before allowing the opponent hanging pawns, it makes sense to have a specific plan in mind for how to restrain them. In diagrams 1a-1c, we see the whole family tree within just three moves.

Like the IQP itself, both of these structures may prove a liability in an endgame. A famous example of the weakness of the isolated pawn couple in an ending is the game Flohr-Vidmar, Nottingham 1936 (diagram 2).

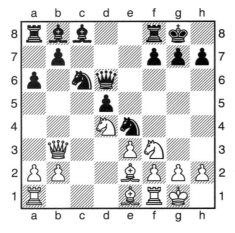

1a) White moves

An exchange of knights on d4 would give White an unpromising symmetrical position, so he exchanges on c6. After 16 ♘xc6 bxc6 (*1b*) Black has an *isolated pawn couple* on c6 and d5.

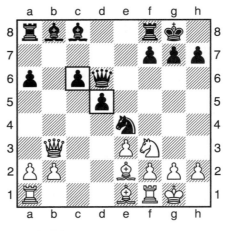

1b) White moves

White provokes ...c5 to weaken the d5-pawn with 17 ♗b4 c5 18 ♗a5 (*1c*), transforming the structure from the isolated pawn couple to the hanging pawns, with pawns on c5 and d5.

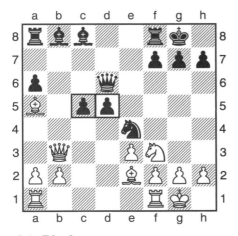

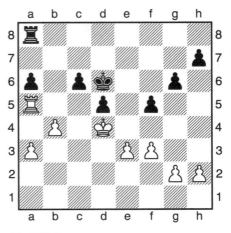

1c) Black moves

Black's hanging pawns are both strong and weak. White must watch out for both ...c4 and ...d4 advances. Black's pawns might prove weak in an endgame, but White faces a tricky middlegame first.

2) White moves

If firmly blockaded, the isolated pawn couple is simply weak. 38 e4! fxe4 39 fxe4 dxe4 40 ♔xe4 destroys the d5-pawn and, with two weak isolated pawns to target as well as active pieces, Flohr won.

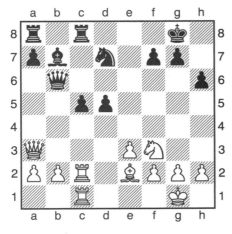

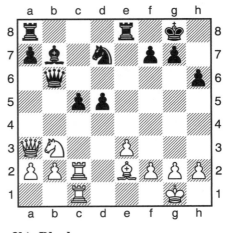

3a) White moves

19 ♘d2! plans ♘b3 and the pin ♗g4, targeting one of the defenders of the c5-pawn. After 19...♖e8 20 ♘b3 (3b), White hopes to induce 20...c4, with 21 ♘d4 to come (see Smart Strategy 20).

3b) Black moves

With 20...d4! Black sacrifices a pawn to activate the bishop on the long diagonal and the e8-rook on the e-file. After 21 ♘xc5 ♘xc5 22 ♖xc5 dxe3 23 fxe3 ♖e7 Black has good compensation.

SMART STRATEGY 18

Pawn-Islands

*Exchange pieces and reach an endgame
with fewer pawn-islands*

A pawn-island means a group of connected pawns. In the initial position both players have one pawn-island each but if, e.g., we removed the f7-pawn from the board, Black would have two pawn-islands. Generally it is an advantage to have fewer pawn-islands than our opponent. It is more difficult to defend each pawn-island when there are fewer pieces on the board, so if we have fewer islands than the opponent, a good strategy is to exchange pieces and head for an endgame. When we discussed the isolated pawn couple and the hanging pawns (Smart Strategy 17) we saw several positions with two pawn-islands vs three. We noted that the possessor of the hanging pawns should create active play for his pieces and avoid the sort of endgame we saw in Flohr-Vidmar. But as always, everything depends on the concrete situation on the board. In diagrams 3a and 3b, the possessor of three pawn-islands has a good position.

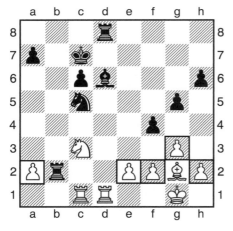

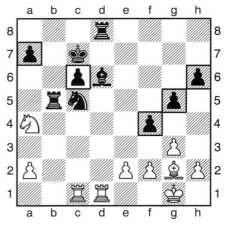

1a) White moves

White has two pawn-islands versus three. 22 ♘a4! exploits the weak c6-pawn. After 22...♘xa4 23 ♖xc6+ ♔b8 24 ♖cxd6 ♖xd6 25 ♖xd6 ♘c3 26 ♗f3! ♘xe2+ 27 ♗xe2 ♖xe2 28 g4! White is better since his rook will harvest black pawns.

1b) White moves

Here Black has met 22 ♘a4 with the stronger defence 22...♖b5!. White now plays 23 ♖c2 with a slight advantage due to his better pawn position. White follows up with a knight manoeuvre to the good outpost c4 via b2.

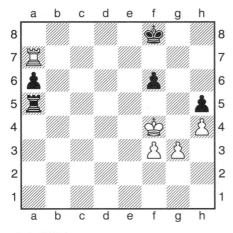

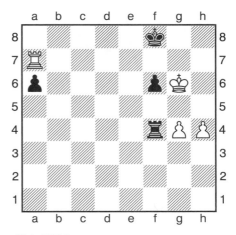

2a) White moves

White has one island vs three, and can advance his pawns without creating weaknesses. After 33 g4! hxg4 34 fxg4 ♖a1? 35 ♔f5 ♖f1+ 36 ♔g6 ♖f4 (*2b*), White has an active king and a passed pawn.

2b) White moves

37 g5! is a strong *pawn-break*. 37...fxg5 38 hxg5 (the pawn protects the king from checks) 38...♖a4 39 ♖a8+ ♔e7 40 ♔h6 a5 41 g6 ♖a1 42 g7 ♖h1+ 43 ♔g6 ♖g1+ 44 ♔h7 ♖h1+ 45 ♔g8 with a simple win.

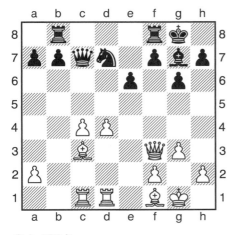

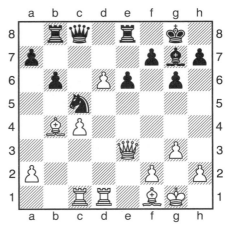

3a) White moves

White has three pawn-islands versus two. But more importantly, he has strong centralized pieces and the *initiative* – i.e. he can create threats. 19 ♗b4 ♖fe8 20 d5! b6 21 d6! ♕c8 22 ♕e3 ♘c5 is diagram 3b.

3b) White moves

You could even say that White has four pawn-islands now since c4 and d6 are dislocated. But White is better thanks to his passed pawn, bishop-pair and active pieces. Attacking with h4-h5 is one idea.

Dominant Knights

Knights are short-range pieces that need outposts

The best possible role for a knight is to stand on a secure square deep in enemy territory where its short-range abilities can cause havoc in the enemy ranks. A strong knight entrenched on our sixth rank often proves a decisive advantage, especially when it prevents the enemy rooks from reaching open files. But it may be possible to work around it – see diagrams 2a and 2b, from the game Lautier-Miles, Biel 1990.

In Smart Strategy 9 we saw the power of a knight on its fifth rank, which typically proves a better piece than the average bishop. Here we take a look at the knight on f5 (a much-loved theme of World Champion Kasparov). From this post it creates dangerous threats against e7, g7 and h6, as we see in the game Capablanca-Fonaroff, New York 1918 (diagram 3).

A knight on the fourth rank can also prove to be exceptionally strong, especially if it is difficult for the opponent to remove it. A famous example is the fifth Petrosian-Botvinnik world championship game in 1963 (diagram 4a).

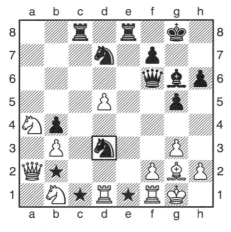

1) White moves

A famous position from the Karpov-Kasparov world championship in 1985. The knight on d3, ably supported by Black's other pieces, paralyses the whole white army. Look at his poor rooks!

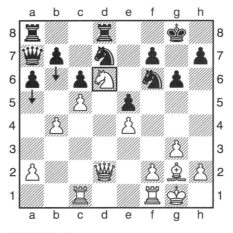

2a) Black moves

Black's rooks are struggling to breathe so he opens new files to escape the super-knight: 19...a5! 20 a3 axb4 21 axb4 b6! 22 ♕c3 bxc5 23 bxc5 ♕a3. Some moves later the position in diagram 2b appeared.

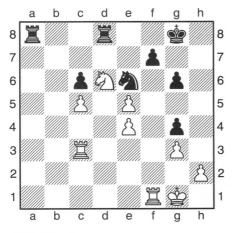

2b) Black moves

With 30...♖d7! Black defends the f7-pawn and prepares a rook manoeuvre to escape the d6-knight. After 31 ♔g2 ♘g5! 32 ♖c2 ♖da7 followed by ...♖a2 or ...♘f3 Black has counterplay.

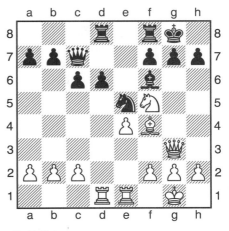

3) White moves

After 17 ♖xd6!? ♖xd6 18 ♗xe5 ♖d1? (18...♕a5! is best) 19 ♖xd1 ♗xe5, White struck with the wonderful tactical sequence 20 ♘h6+ ♔h8 21 ♕xe5! ♕xe5 22 ♘xf7+ 1-0. What a super knight!

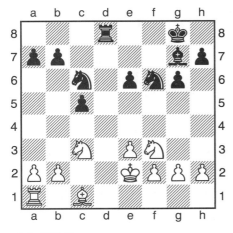

4a) White moves

15 ♘g5! ♖e8 16 ♘ge4! secures an 'eternal' knight with pressure on the c5-pawn. After 16...♘xe4 17 ♘xe4 b6 18 ♖b1 ♘b4 19 ♗d2 ♘d5 20 a4 ♖c8 21 b3 ♗f8 22 ♖c1 ♗e7 23 b4! the pressure is increased.

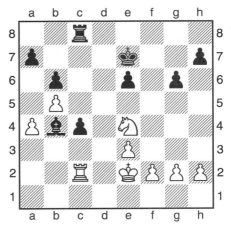

4b) White moves

Some moves later, the versatile knight attacked the c-pawn with 29 ♘d2! c3 (also bad is 29...♗xd2 30 ♔xd2 ♔d6 31 ♔c3) 30 ♘e4 ♗a5 31 ♔d3 ♖d8+ 32 ♔c4 and White won the pawn.

49

SMART STRATEGY 20 — Creating an Outpost for a Knight

Play clever with the pawns!

Outposts often arise quite naturally from the pawn-structure, but in other cases we need to put in some work to create them. As a simple example, we might make some pawn exchanges that give the opponent an isolated pawn (see Smart Strategy 16) so that we can put a knight on the blockading square in front of it. Or in Strategy 19, Petrosian had earlier exchanged on e6 to create a strong-point on e4 for his knight.

Here we shall be looking at more elaborate methods. 'Philidor's Ring' was one of the earliest examples of a player deliberately eking out an outpost for a knight. Black uses two pawns and a knight for this operation. Our example comes from a 1783 game by Philidor, a French master who emphasized the key role of pawns in chess.

Another method (diagram 2a) is to advance a pawn to the fifth rank followed by establishing an outpost on the sixth rank. Lastly we look (in diagram 3a) at how to plug an outpost from the defender's point of view.

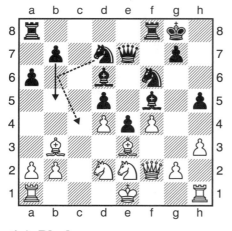

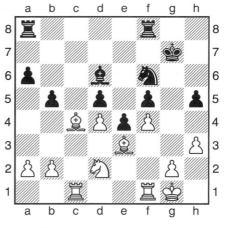

1a) Black moves

Philidor's Ring is obtained by 17...b5! 18 0-0 ♘b6!. After 19 ♘g3 g6 20 ♖ac1 ♘c4! (plugging the c-file) 21 ♘xf5 gxf5 22 ♕g3+ ♕g7 23 ♕xg7+ ♔xg7 24 ♗xc4 *(1b)* Black has an important decision.

1b) Black moves

Black has a massive advantage after 24...dxc4!, which creates a superb outpost on d5 for the f6-knight. Instead Philidor played 24...bxc4? but after 25 b3 White's position was only a little worse.

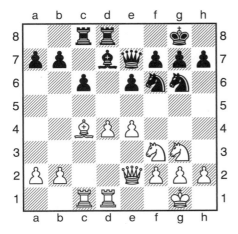

2a) White moves

1 e5 creates an outpost on d6 but gives Black one on d5. As White's outpost is further up the board, it is worth more than Black's. 1...♘d5 2 ♘e4 ♖c7 3 g3! ♗e8 4 ♘d6 ♘b6 5 ♗b3 ♘c8 (2b).

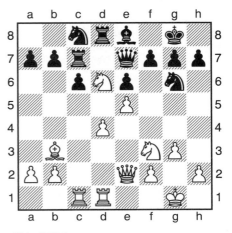

2b) White moves

Black wants to neutralize the outpost but this slow manoeuvre has put the knight on a poor square. After 6 ♘e4! White's knight is very active, eyeing d6, c5 and potentially f6. Compare all four knights!

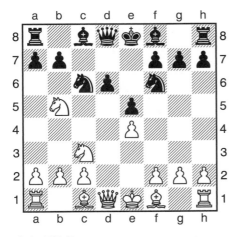

3a) White moves

A standard position from the Sicilian Pelikan/Sveshnikov. If 7 ♘d5 Black plugs the outpost by 7...♘xd5 8 exd5 (8 ♕xd5? a6 leaves the queen misplaced: 9 ♘a3 ♗e6) 8...♘e7, when he has few problems.

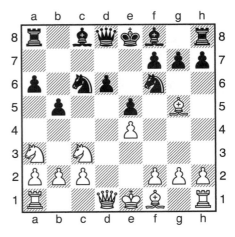

3b) White moves

Here 7 ♗g5! a6 8 ♘a3 b5 has been played. After 9 ♗xf6 gxf6 10 ♘d5 f5 White has a knight on d5, which is more influential than a pawn on that square. But Black has active counterplay.

<table>
<tr>
<td>
</td>
<td>
Dominating the Knight
</td>
</tr>
</table>

Restrict the knight with your pawns or pieces

When we talk of a piece being 'dominated', we mean that it can't move without being taken. Even if this piece can't be captured, its paralysis can have a devastating effect.

The piece most prone to being dominated is the knight, due to the relatively small number of squares to which it can move, especially when close to the edges or corners. In diagram 1, a single centralized bishop traps a knight on the edge of the board. In diagram 2, a knight dominates a bishop in a similar way, albeit with the help of an additional obstruction. The rook can control all four escape-squares of a knight on b2, b7, g2 or g7 (see diagram 3). Even pawns and kings can get in on the action. A king can trap a knight on a corner square, while the knight is notoriously bad at halting rook's pawns (see diagram 4). In the middlegame, well-placed pawns can be used to kill a knight's aggressive plans. For instance, a pawn on g3 prevents ...♘f4 by a knight on h5. In diagram 5, two pawns keep a knight passive for many moves.

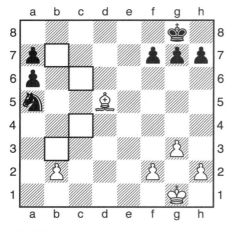

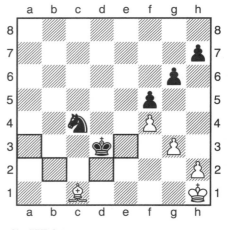

1) Black moves

A typical way for a bishop to dominate a knight on the edge of the board: it controls the four squares where it could legally move. Black has no defence against White's threat of b4, winning the knight.

2) White moves

Now it is the knight that dominates the enemy bishop. Thanks to the white pawn fixed on f4, there are no squares available to the bishop, and Black will play ...♚c2 and take the bishop.

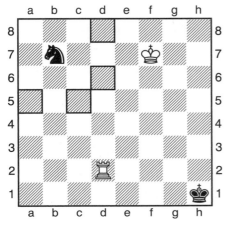

3) White moves

1 ♖d5! is the key move to control all four of the knight's escape-squares. After 1...♔g2 2 ♔e7 ♔f3 the simplest is 3 ♖b5, picking up the knight since the king now controls d6 and d8.

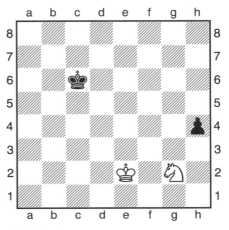

4) Black moves

At first sight it isn't obvious how Black might hope to win here, but after 1...h3, White has no way to stop the pawn queening. If the knight weren't on the board at all, it would be a draw!

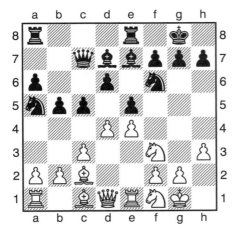

5) White moves

14 b3 prevents ...♘c4-b6 and prepares 15 d5, which keeps the a5-knight from playing a role in the fight for the centre. Even after ...♘b7-d8 the d5-pawn will stop the knight becoming active.

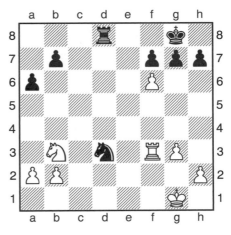

6) Black moves

In this game from the 2015 Swedish Championship, Black played the clever 36...b6!, not allowing ♘c5 after ...♘xb2. The game continued 37 ♘d2 ♘xb2 38 ♘e4 ♘c4!, with an advantage for Black.

The Superfluous Knight

When you have a good square for a piece,
but two pieces that want it...

The 'superfluous piece' is an expression coined by the famous Russian chess coach Mark Dvoretsky. It describes a situation where two pieces both want to use the same square, and otherwise lack good posts. Only one of them can actually sit on this square, which leaves the other piece short of good squares. The ideal solution is to exchange off one of the pieces so that the other can sit pretty on the cherished square, but an alert opponent will seek to prevent this plan.

In our first position below the knight on c3 cannot occupy d5, because the other knight has already done so. The superfluous knight is jealously dreaming about that d5-square! White would like to exchange the d5-knight for the enemy knight, but Black neatly sidesteps and the white knights end up treading on each other's toes.

An example of a superfluous bishop can be found in diagram 4 of Smart Strategy 25, where the f4-bishop would like to settle on e5, but the e5-knight is in the way.

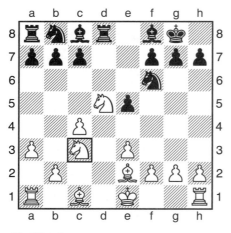

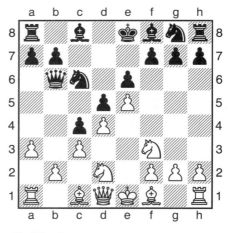

1) Black moves

White's c3-knight is superfluous, and also in the way of the d5-knight. After the nice retreat 11...♘e8! followed by 12...c6, two knights are 'killed' with one blow, and must retreat in disarray.

2) Black moves

In this opening position (an Advance French), Black's kingside minor pieces both want the e7-square. Note that there are some tactical issues too: 7...♘ge7? loses to 8 ♗xc4! dxc4 9 ♘xc4 and ♘d6+.

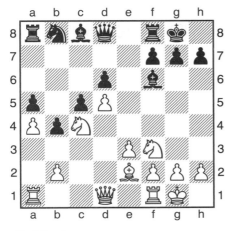

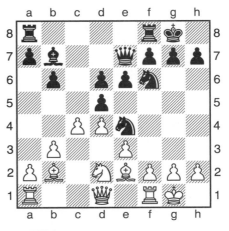

3) Black moves

In a game between two experienced grandmasters, Black chose 13...♗a6?!, but an exchange on c4 would just help White arrange his forces. 13...♗b7 is better, leaving the e2-bishop superfluous.

4) White moves

In this position from a famous 19th-century game, the chess trainer Dvoretsky pointed out the instructive 13 ♘b1!, leaving the f6-knight superfluous, and planning to take over the centre with f3.

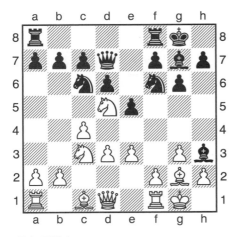

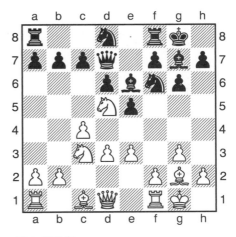

5a) White moves

Here the c3-knight can disturb the harmony in Black's position with 11 ♘xf6+! ♗xf6 12 ♘d5, forcing the defensive 12...♗d8 since the black queen is overloaded by the need to protect h3 and c7.

5b) White moves

Black has just played 10...♘d8!, avoiding the problems we saw in diagram 5a. If now 11 ♘xf6+ ♗xf6 12 ♘d5?! (12 ♗d2 is better) 12...♗g7 the knight on d5 has problems since ...c6 will follow.

Bishop against Knight

*The bishop likes an open board;
the knight prefers blocked play with outposts*

Although the knight and bishop are considered roughly equal in value, they have very different strengths and weaknesses. The knight vs bishop imbalance is one of the most important in chess strategy.

The bishop performs best when the position is open, and it is not obstructed by pawns. Thanks to its long-range capabilities the bishop really shows its teeth when there is play on both wings. The knight is almost the complete opposite, preferring a blocked position with secure outposts and play focused in a small sector, such as one wing or a central area.

We shall look at three good positions for the bishop and three good positions for the knight. The first two constructed positions are from the famous book by Capablanca, *Chess Fundamentals*. The two others are from the games Poletaev-Flohr, Moscow 1951 and Capablanca-Reshevsky, Nottingham 1936. The first of these practical examples demonstrates a strong bishop versus a knight lacking an outpost while the latter demonstrates the good knight versus a bad bishop obstructed by its own pawns.

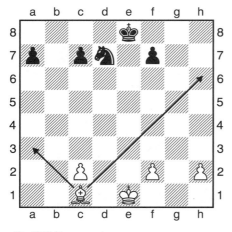

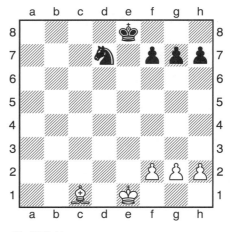

1) White moves

The c1-bishop supports the h-pawn while at the same time controlling the a3-square in front of the enemy passed pawn. The black knight cannot do likewise and the bishop is therefore stronger.

2) White moves

Here there is only play on one side of the board, and that benefits the knight. The bishop can't show its full strength since half the board is empty. But neither side has real winning chances.

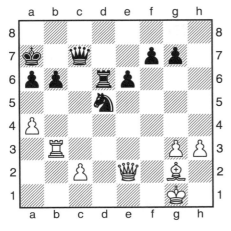

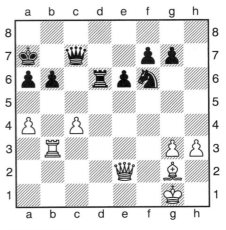

3a) White moves

1 c4! dislodges the d5-knight. 1...♘e7 2 ♕f3 ♕c6? (2...♘c6 3 a5 bxa5 4 ♕f2+ ♘d4 5 ♖b7+ and White should win) 3 ♕xf7 ♕c5+ 4 ♔h2 ♖d1 5 ♖e3! b5 6 ♕xe6 ♘c8 7 a5! ♕c7 8 ♕e4 ♕b8 9 ♕c6!, mating.

3b) White moves

Black has played 1...♘f6 intending ...e5-e4, blocking the g2-bishop. But after 2 ♕f3! ♖c8 3 a5! e5 4 ♕e3 ♘d7 5 axb6+ ♖xb6 6 ♖xb6 ♘xb6 7 ♕xe5 ♘xc4 8 ♕d4+ ♘b6 9 ♕xg7 the h-pawn is very fast.

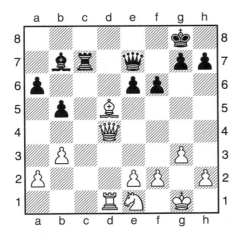

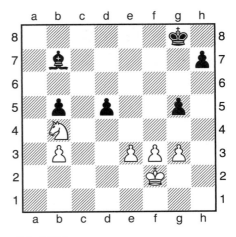

4a) Black moves

The best recapture is 27...♗xd5 (Black played 27...exd5?). After 28 f3 ♖d7 29 ♕c3 e5 30 ♘d3 the minor pieces have equal value. The knight has a stable outpost on c5 and the bishop is centralized.

4b) White moves

41 g4! prevents ...h5-h4, which would be dangerous in combination with a bishop. 41...♔g7 42 ♔e2 ♔g6? 43 ♔d3 h5 44 gxh5+ ♔xh5 45 ♔d4 ♔h4 46 ♘xd5 ♔g3 47 f4 and White won.

Open Diagonals

Like a rapid-transit system for a bishop straight into the enemy position

A bishop with open diagonals can prove a tremendous piece, readily coordinating with other attacking forces. When there is no enemy bishop moving on the same coloured squares, its power is even greater, as there is nothing to neutralize it. Open diagonals are the air the bishop breathes, just like the rook needs open files and the knight depends on outposts to work effectively.

In Smart Strategy 1 we mentioned the a2-g8 diagonal. Many games have been decided by an attack on the weak point f7. When our opponent has castled kingside, the b1-h7 diagonal is often useful to control. Diagrams 4a and 4b (from a game the author won against Tisdall) show how one can step up the pressure on the diagonal by placing the queen behind the bishop or (aggressively) in front of the bishop. In the first four diagrams we examine play on the two *long diagonals* – that is, the two that run through the very centre of the board. The importance of these diagonals is one reason why the *fianchetto* is a popular way to develop a bishop.

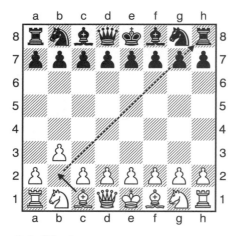

1a) Black moves

White can control the long dark diagonal toward Black's centre and kingside after only two moves with 1 b3 followed by 2 ♗b2 (i.e. a fianchetto). How does Black counteract this dangerous plan?

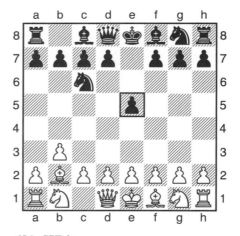

1b) White moves

Black has played 1...e5 2 ♗b2 ♘c6, which is probably the strongest set-up to parry White's kingside ambitions. White must be content with pressure on e5 after, for instance, 3 e3 d5 4 ♗b5 ♗d6 5 f4.

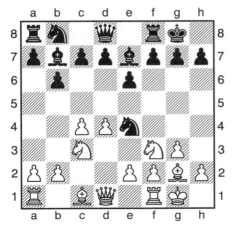

2) White moves

Another way to parry our opponent's plan of controlling the long diagonal is to develop the bishop to the same diagonal and neutralize it. Here 8 ♘xe4 ♗xe4 9 ♘h4 ♗xg2 10 ♘xg2 even exchanges it.

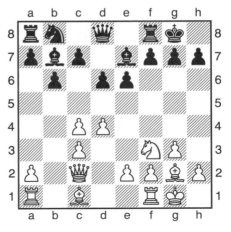

3) White moves

A potential drawback with a queenside fianchetto is that the bishop is undefended. Here it is exploited by the tactical trick 10 ♘g5!, threatening mate. After 10...♗xg5 11 ♗xb7 White wins material.

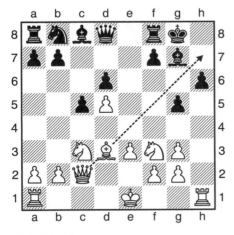

4a) Black moves

13...f5 obstructs the b1-h7 diagonal with a pawn. After 14 0-0 ♕f6 White can re-open it by 15 e4! fxe4?! (developing the knight is preferable) 16 ♘xe4, with good central control and attacking chances.

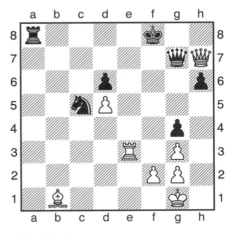

4b) White moves

White is still doubled on the diagonal, but with the queen now taking the leading role. 36 ♕f5+ ♔g8 37 ♕f4 ♖d8 38 ♗f5! provoked 38...h5 39 ♗c2! ♔h8. After 40 ♕f5! Black is lost as h5 falls.

Good and Bad Bishops

Exchange the bad bishop for the opponent's good one!

Bishops are formally termed 'good' and 'bad' based on how obstructed they are by fixed pawns in the centre. While these are useful indications of how effective each bishop will be, it is not too uncommon for a 'bad' bishop to be a good piece, and vice versa.

A light-squared bishop is 'good' is there aren't *friendly* pawns fixed on light squares in the centre, and 'bad' if there are (and in that case, the dark-squared bishop is 'good'). And so on.

It is normally good strategy to exchange a bad bishop for the opponent's good bishop. How good and bad bishops measure up against knights always depends on the specifics of each position. If we can put our bad bishop outside the pawn-chain, then it will be much more active, and the opponent may find it necessary to exchange if off. But note that, if its way back is cut off, the bishop may be in danger of getting trapped.

It is important to think about bad and good bishops when we are deciding what kind of pawn-formation to set up in the centre.

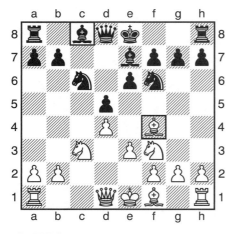

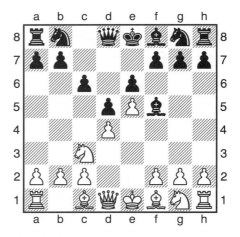

1) White moves

The f4-bishop is a bad bishop outside the pawn-chain and controls the centre. The c8-bishop is a bad bishop but defends the queenside well. 8 h3 preserves the bishop from exchange by 8...♘h5.

2) White moves

The f5-bishop is actively placed outside the pawn-chain. White can seek to exploit its shortage of squares by 5 g4 ♗g6 6 ♘ge2 intending h4 and ♘f4, hoping to open lines and attack on the kingside.

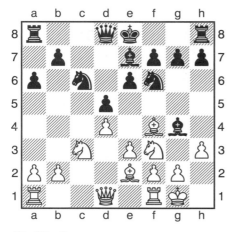

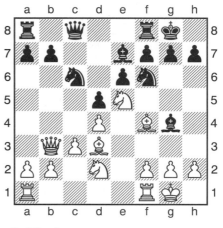

3) Black moves

A classic decision. 10...♗xf3 11 ♗xf3 leaves Black solid but passive. 10...♗h5 is more ambitious. After 11 ♘e5 ♗xe2 12 ♕xe2 ♖c8 Black has the better bishop, but White's pieces are more active.

4) Black moves

11...♘xe5 12 ♗xe5 helps the superfluous f4-bishop, while 11...♗f5 allows White to break up Black's pawns. 11...♗h5, planning ...♗g6, is best. After 12 ♕c2 ♗d6! 13 ♗g3 ♕c7 14 ♘df3 ♗g6 Black is fine.

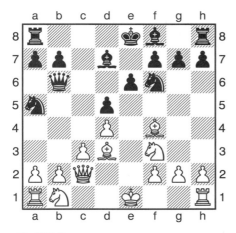

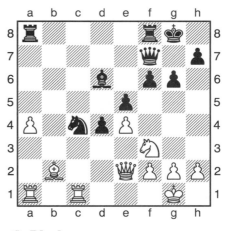

5) White moves

This is a Fischer-Petrosian game from 1970. 11 a4! prevented 11...♗b5 and so kept White's good bishop. This is an improvement over 11 ♘bd2 ♗b5!, as played in earlier games.

6) Black moves

28...♘xb2!? exchanges a good-looking knight for an inactive bishop. But after 29 ♕xb2 ♖fb8 30 ♕a2 ♗b4 Black's bishop on c3 will be stronger than the knight. A 'bad' bishop but a good piece!

SMART STRATEGY 26   Opposite-Coloured Bishops

Both players are a piece up and a piece down!

A bishop can only move to half the squares on the board: a light-squared bishop can never move to a dark square, and vice versa. That means that if the two players have opposite-coloured bishops, these two pieces move in different universes. This has a profound effect on the strategy. Both players are a piece down on a particular colour! The initiative therefore has an even greater role than normal: if we can make a series of threats on 'our' coloured squares, then the opponent will be poorly placed to parry them. In Adams-Navara, Biel 2015 (diagrams 4a and 4b), we see White setting up threats on the light squares before his opponent can make anything of his domination of the dark squares.

We start with two positions that show the well-known drawish tendencies of *pure* opposite-coloured bishop endings. Once a blockade is set up, the stronger side may lack the resources to break it. But remember that once a few extra pieces are added – one pair of rooks may be enough – it is the initiative that counts!

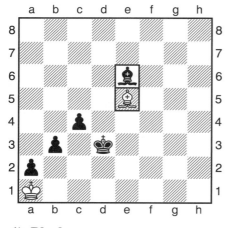

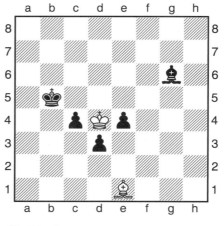

1) Black moves

Black has three extra pawns but cannot win because of the opposite-coloured bishops and the white king's location in the corner. 1...c3 2 ♗xc3! ♔xc3 is stalemate, and there is no other way forward.

2) Black moves

Black must be accurate to win. 1...♗a4!! threatens ...♔b3 and ...c3. 2 ♔xc4 e3 3 ♔c3 ♗a3 is *zugzwang* – White must self-destruct because the rules of chess don't allow him to pass. 4...d2 will win.

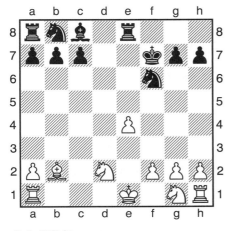

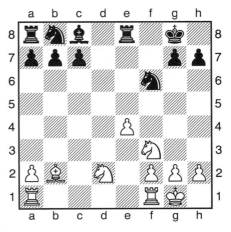

3a) White moves

The c8-bishop has little to do on the c8-h3 diagonal, while the b2-bishop coordinates with the white knights after 11 ♘gf3! since 11...♘xe4? loses material after 12 ♘e5+. Better is 11...♔g8 12 0-0 *(3b)*.

3b) Black moves

Now 12...♘xe4? gives White the initiative after 13 ♘xe4 ♖xe4 14 ♖fe1 ♗f5! 15 ♘d4 ♖xe1+ 16 ♖xe1 ♗g6 17 ♖e7. Black should seek play on 'his' light squares by 12...b6 and ...♗b7 with pressure on e4.

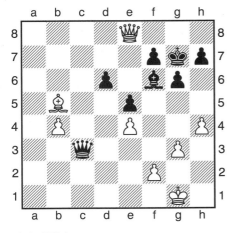

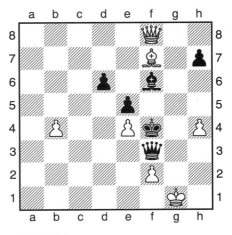

4a) White moves

After 29 ♗c6! ♕f3!? 30 ♕d7! (not 30 ♗d5? ♗xh4! 31 gxh4 ♕g4+ forcing perpetual check) 30...g5 Adams should have played 31 ♗d5!; for instance, 31...♕h5 32 g4 ♕g6 33 h5 and f7 falls.

4b) White moves

The position after the further moves 31...gxh4 32 ♕xf7+ ♔h6 33 ♕f8+ ♔h5 34 ♗f7+ ♔g5 35 gxh4+ ♔f4. Now 36 ♗e6!! wins. 36...♔xe4 covers the bishop but 37 ♗d5+! ♔xd5 38 ♕a8+ wins the queen.

Restricting the Bishop with the Pawns

Place your pawns to limit your opponent's bishop

We have already seen that pawns make sturdy and stable diagonal chains, so it is no surprise that they can be used to restrict the diagonal-moving bishop. For instance, after 1 g3 d5 2 ♗g2 c6 (diagram 1a) the three-pawn chain b7-d5 restricts White's light-squared bishop. Instead 2...c5 would have given Black a more active position in the centre but White's bishop would have had much softer targets on the long diagonal. It is a matter of taste how to play since there are pros and cons with all strategies in chess.

In diagrams 2a and 2b we examine the Stonewall set-up, where Black arranges his four most central pawns in a way that restricts both the black and white light-squared bishops. Even though White's bishop is formally 'good', both pieces have trouble becoming active.

An important strategy to immobilize a bishop was demonstrated by Capablanca as Black in a famous game against Winter (see diagrams 3a and 3b). This way of shutting a bishop totally out of the game can be used in many similar situations, and often proves decisive.

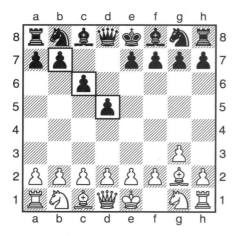

1a) White moves

Three black pawns blunt the g2-bishop's influence on the long light-square diagonal, giving Black a firm central foothold. After 3 ♘f3 ♘f6 4 0-0 ♗f5 5 d4 e6 6 c4 ♘bd7 7 ♘c3 h6 we have diagram 1b.

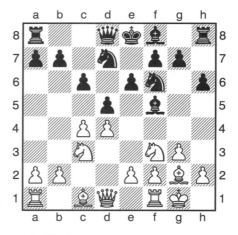

1b) White moves

White can eliminate the strong d5-pawn with the knight manoeuvre 8 ♘d2 followed by e4. After 8...♗e7 9 e4 dxe4 10 ♘dxe4 White's g2-bishop is improved as well as the central situation.

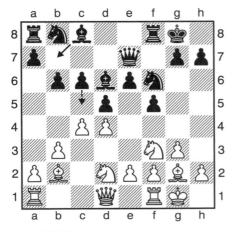

2a) White moves

In a Stonewall, Black has just played 9...b6, planning to activate the bad bishop with ...♗b7 followed by a later ...c5, when the bishop will influence the game in the centre.

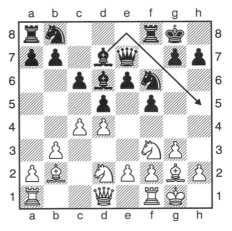

2b) White moves

Here 9...♗d7 has been played, introducing the typical manoeuvre ...♗e8-h5, when the bad bishop is outside the pawn-chain and exerts pressure on the h5-d1 diagonal. However, this is a slow plan.

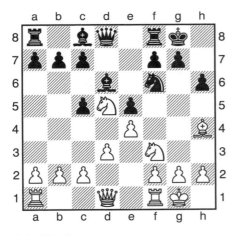

3a) Black moves

Capablanca played 10...g5!, harassing the bishop and unpinning the knight. 11 ♘xf6+ (crucially, 11 ♘xg5 ♘xd5! costs White a piece) 11...♕xf6 12 ♗g3 ♗g4 13 h3 ♗xf3 14 ♕xf3 ♕xf3 15 gxf3 f6 *(3b)*.

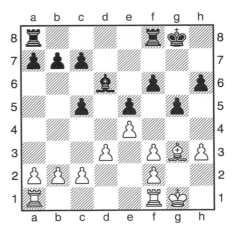

3b) White moves

The g3-bishop is sealed in by the pawns. Black plans to attack on the queenside, where he practically has an extra piece. The 'bad' d6-bishop is better than the 'good' g3-bishop, which can't break free.

If you have the two bishops, seek an open position

When chess-players talk about the 'bishop-pair', they generally mean a position where one player has two bishops, while the opponent has either two knights or a bishop and a knight. Material is equal, so why is it 'an advantage'? It's because two bishops complement each other perfectly. They control squares of both colours, and if a pawn (or king...) escapes the gaze of one bishop, it tends to walk into the teeth of the other one. The bishop-pair is particularly effective in open positions, as this means more open diagonals and fewer places to hide. So if you trade a bishop for a knight early in the game, you should try to keep the position closed or blocked since this stifles the bishops and allows the knight to shine. The bishop-pair isn't always an advantage – it depends on the structure and how effective each piece is.

A famous example of the bishop-pair in an open position is Englisch-Steinitz, London 1883, which we shall examine in diagrams 2a-2e. Steinitz used a three-step plan to immobilize the opponent's knight, and in turn his bishop as well!

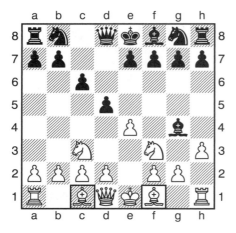

1) Black moves

Black must decide whether to keep the bishop or exchange it. The most solid course is 4...♗xf3 5 ♕xf3 e6, keeping the centre closed. It will be hard work for White to put his bishops to good use.

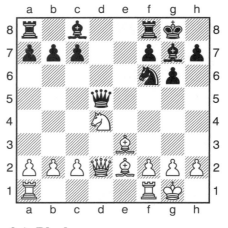

2a) Black moves

The centre is open so Steinitz grabbed the bishop-pair with 12...♘g4!, threatening ...♘xe3. White parted with his light-squared bishop with 13 ♗xg4 ♗xg4 and played 14 ♘b3, leading to diagram 2b.

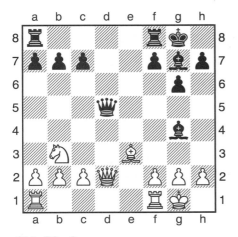

2b) Black moves

14...♕c4 15 c3 ♖ad8 is tempting, targeting the queen. But a clearer strategy is to reach an endgame where the bishop-pair is a big plus. Steinitz played 14...♕xd2 15 ♘xd2 ♖ad8 16 c3 ♖fe8 17 ♘b3 *(2c)*.

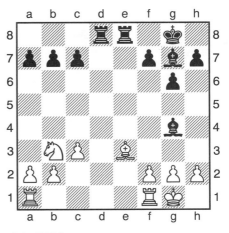

2c) White moves

The first step in the plan is restricting the knight by 17...b6!. After 18 h3 ♗e6, 19 ♘d4 would be met by 19...♗d5, but 19 ♖fd1 c5! started to put both the knight *and* the bishop into straitjackets.

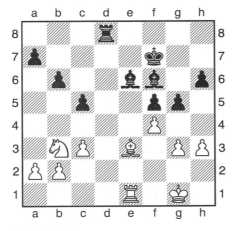

2d) Black moves

Some moves later, Steinitz is using his kingside pawns to deprive the bishop of squares. The next step is to drive the knight into passivity: 27...a5 28 ♘c1 a4! 29 a3 ♗c4 (domination!) 30 ♔f2 *(2e)*.

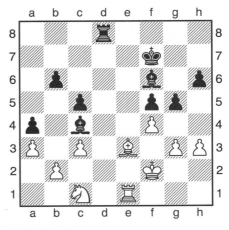

2e) Black moves

Step 3: breakthrough. 30...♖d5 and ...b5-b4 is one way. Or, even stronger, 30...g4! 31 hxg4 fxg4 32 ♖h1 ♖h8 and ...h5-h4. White is busted. In the game, Steinitz won by slightly more complex means.

Rooks are great at exerting pressure along files

An open file is one on which there are no pawns at all, while a half-open file contains only a white or a black pawn. They can arise from pawn exchanges (giving both sides a half-open file) a pawn recapturing a piece or a pawn sacrifice – in these last two cases giving only one side a half-open file. An open file can be an invasion route for either side, or a location for exchanges of queens and rooks. A half-open file is different, as it can only be used by one side. The main theme is *pressure*, which can be stepped up by bringing a knight to an outpost on the file, and with pawn-breaks acting like battering-rams against the enemy pawn that sits on the half-open file.

We have already seen examples on this theme in Smart Strategy 15, where we looked at doubled pawns. In diagrams 4 and 5 we see pawn-breaks being used to open files. In the last position, Kramnik-Nisipeanu, Dortmund 2015, Kramnik abandoned the open c-file because Black had no *entry-squares* on this file – all the key squares were covered, so the black rook could not penetrate.

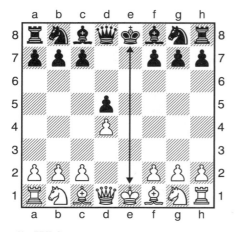

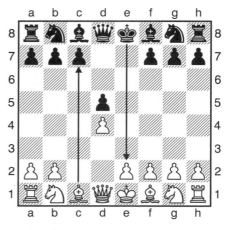

1) White moves

The e-file is open, so it is in both players' interest to place a rook, or sometimes both rooks, on the e-file to exercise central pressure. This will tend to result in exchanges. The game lacks imbalance.

2) White moves

A slight difference in the pawns means a huge difference! White can exert pressure on the c-file, Black on the e-file. There's no natural path for rook exchanges, and an unbalanced struggle lies ahead.

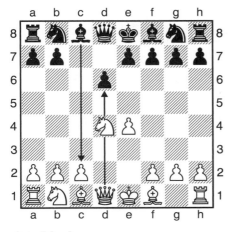

3a) Black moves

A Sicilian Defence. Black will generally place a rook on the c-file, which will play a major role in any counterattacking plan. White will seek to dominate the centre, with d-file pressure a major theme.

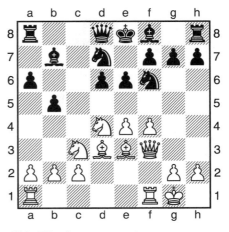

3b) Black moves

10...♘c5 blocks the c-file, so 10...♖c8! is more accurate. Then 11 g4?! is reckless since Black has the positional exchange sacrifice (Smart Strategy 41) 11...♖xc3!? 12 bxc3 ♘c5, with pressure on e4.

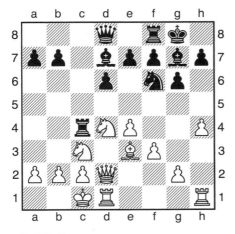

4) White moves

White can open a file on the kingside in two ways: the pawn sacrifice 14 h5 ♘xh5 15 g4 or 14 g4, preparing the break h5. If Black stops it with 14...h5 then 15 gxh5 ♘xh5 gives White a half-open g-file.

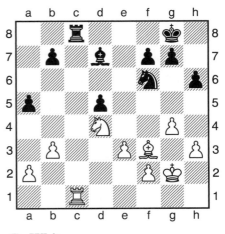

5) White moves

27 ♖b1 avoids the exchange of rooks and prepares the possible opening of a new file with the pawn-break b4, putting pressure on the exposed b7-pawn. The black rook can achieve little on the c-file.

Play on the Ranks

Remember that rooks also move horizontally

To get the most out of your rooks, you must learn how to use them along the ranks. Bringing a rook to the seventh rank is often a major strategic goal because of the vulnerable unmoved pawns that tend to sit on this rank, and the fact that there may also be threats to the enemy king. However, if a rook only has a few squares available to it on the seventh rank, it may be possible for the defender to eject it using his king (see diagram 2).

In diagram 3, we examine a case where White is able to use a rook to good effect along his fifth rank, putting pressure on an array of pawns. A rook can also operate along a rank to attack pawns from the front; repeated frontal attacks against a row of pawns will loosen them up and create weaknesses of one type of another. Diagrams 4a and 4b feature a famous Marshall-Lasker game from their 1907 world championship match. Lasker uses his rook on both his fourth and third ranks. Diagram 5 comes from a Keres-Petrosian game in the 1959 Candidates tournament. Petrosian used the ranks to manoeuvre for both attacking and defensive purposes.

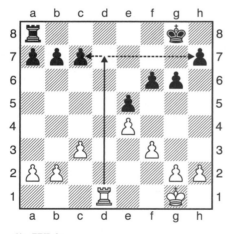

1) White moves

White gains a huge advantage by placing his rook on the seventh rank with 1 ♖d7. Black is paralysed as he cannot activate his pieces or remove the white rook without losing at least one of his pawns.

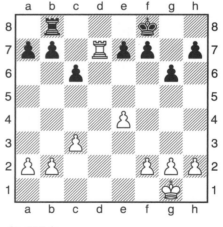

2) White moves

Here the rook looks good on the seventh rank, but actually achieves nothing and will be forced back. For example, 1 ♔f1 ♔e8 2 ♖d2 (2 ♖c7?? ♔d8 leaves the rook trapped) 2...♖d8 with an equal ending.

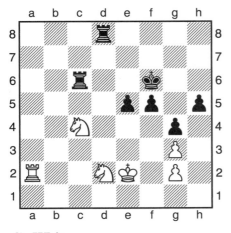

3) White moves

In this game from a Swedish tournament, 70 ♖a5! was met by 70...♖d4, also using his fifth rank. With 71 ♖xe5! ♖xd2+ 72 ♔xd2 ♖xc4 73 ♖e8 ♖e4 74 ♖xe4 fxe4 75 ♔e3 White could have held the draw.

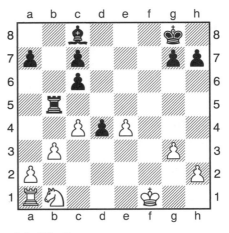

4a) Black moves

Lasker continued 21...♖h5! 22 ♔g1 (22 h4 g5 23 hxg5? ♖h1+ with a deadly pin on White's first rank) 22...c5! (opening the third rank for his rook) 23 ♘d2 ♔f7 24 ♖f1+ ♔e7 25 a3 (4b).

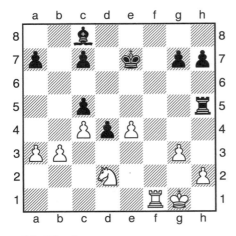

4b) Black moves

Lasker now switched his rook to the other wing, stretching White's defences: 25...♖h6! 26 h4 ♖a6! 27 ♖a1 ♗g4 28 ♔f2 ♔e6 29 a4 ♔e5 30 ♔g2 ♖f6!, cutting off the king, and he won with ...d3 and ...♔d4.

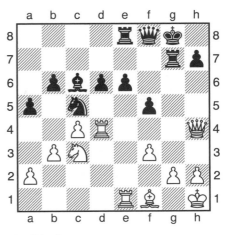

5) Black moves

Petrosian played 34...♖g6!, controlling the third rank and planning to double rooks on the g-file. 35 ♖d2 ♖d8 36 ♖ed1 ♖d7! 37 ♕f2 ♕d8 38 ♕e3 e5 and ...♖dg7 is coming, with good kingside play.

SMART STRATEGY 31

The Rook-Lift

Bring the rook into the attack in front of your pawns

A rook-lift is a manoeuvre by a rook along a rank in front of a row of pawns. The idea is normally to bring it into an attack on the enemy king. This is a valuable idea in positions where it is hard to open a file by normal means or doing so would be too weakening.

Indeed, a rook-lift has a similar effect to opening a file, but without using the pawns. However, it doesn't come free of charge. It takes a few moves to bring the rook into position, and if the attack fails, the rook can be left poorly placed in front of the pawns. And while a rook-lift is a way to avoid weakening your own pawns, if the rook is to move freely along the third rank, then the pawns must remain on their second rank. This may leave a weak back rank – which one rook has already left. So a rook-lift is a major *commitment* that should only be undertaken if we are sure it is truly effective.

A famous example is Alekhine-Kmoch, San Remo 1930 (diagrams 1a-1d) where Alekhine successfully activated two rooks in front of his kingside pawns. Diagrams 2a and 2b are also instructive.

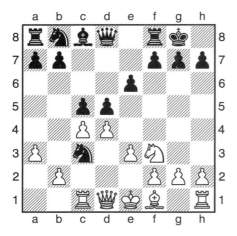

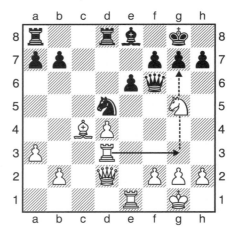

1a) White moves

With 10 ♖xc3 the activation of the rook begins. 10...cxd4 11 exd4 ♘c6 12 ♗e2 dxc4 13 ♗xc4 ♕f6 14 0-0 ♖d8 15 ♖d3 (defending the IQP) 15...♗d7 16 ♖e1 ♗e8 17 ♕d2 ♘e7 18 ♘g5 ♘d5 (*1b*).

1b) White moves

19 ♖f3 ♕e7 20 ♖g3 activates the rook. It defends the g5-knight and eyes g7. Alekhine is seeking to provoke dark-square weaknesses with 21 ♕d3 g6. Now 20...h6 21 ♘f3 ♕f6 brings us to diagram 1c.

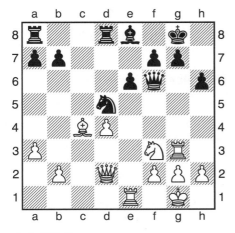

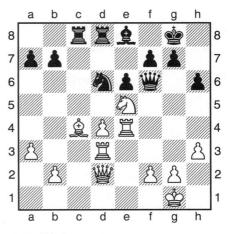

1c) White moves

22 ♖e4 activates the rook on the fourth rank but weakens White's back rank. After 22...♘e7! 23 ♘e5 (23 ♖eg4? ♘f5) 23...♘f5 24 ♖d3 ♖ac8 25 h3 ♘d6! (*1d*) the game is balanced on a knife edge.

1d) White moves

26 ♖f4 ♘xc4 27 ♘xc4 ♕g5 (27...♕e7!?) 28 ♖g3! (attack!) 28...♕d5 29 ♘e3 ♕c6 30 ♔h2 ♕c1? (30...♕d6! 31 ♖fg4 g6 32 ♖h4 h5 holds the balance) 31 ♕b4! ♕c7 32 d5! and White's attack crashed through.

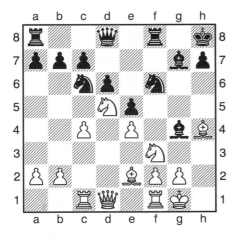

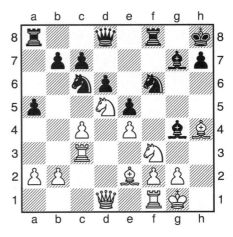

2a) White moves

The idea of 18 ♖c3! is to transfer the rook to the kingside after 18...♗xf3 (for 18...a5 see diagram 2b) 19 ♖xf3 ♘d4 20 ♖h3. This is Engqvist-Johansson, Swedish Ch, Helsingborg 1991.

2b) White moves

White would now have activated the rook on the queenside with 19 ♖b3!. After 19...b6 20 ♖d3! there will follow a3 and b4, while after 19...♖b8 20 ♖d3! he has the idea of 21 c5.

Handling the Major Pieces

The queen and rooks require special treatment

In the opening, we normally move some of the central pawns followed by the knights and bishops. After this initial development, the next priority is to ensure the safety of the king by castling, which also brings a rook into play. Sometimes this leaves the rook somewhat inactively sitting behind the f-pawn, but it is a step closer to becoming active, either by a move to a central file or thanks to an advance by the f-pawn. We may also improve the queen's location if we can do so without exposing it to attack. The queen's rook is the piece we normally develop last. This important final step of the development plan should not be forgotten.

How the major pieces are then deployed will depend on the strategic direction the game takes. Sometimes a file is so important that we want to place the maximum force on it by tripling our major pieces. This works best if the queen is at the rear, with the two rooks in front. This set-up is called the Alekhine Gun, the stem game being Alekhine-Nimzowitsch, San Remo 1930 (see diagram 2).

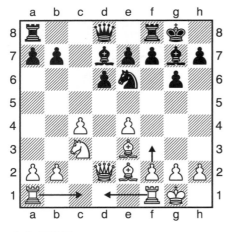

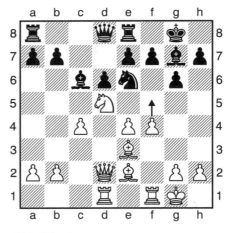

1a) White moves

White can consolidate his space advantage by 13 ♖ac1, with 14 ♖fd1 and 15 f3 in mind. This conservative positional approach seeks to reduce Black's counterplay to a minimum by offering no targets.

1b) Black moves

This is Larsen-Petrosian, Santa Monica 1966. White has adopted a more aggressive set-up, with the rook staying on f1 to support the f4-f5 advance, harassing the black knight while eyeing the f7-square.

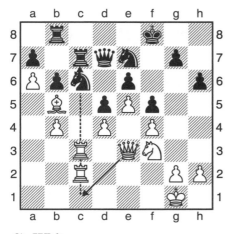

2) White moves

Alekhine loaded his 'Gun' with 26 ♕c1!. After 26...♖bc8 27 ♗a4 b5 28 ♗xb5 ♔e8 29 ♗a4 ♔d8 30 h4 Black is in zugzwang: the decisive move b5 will follow after a black king move.

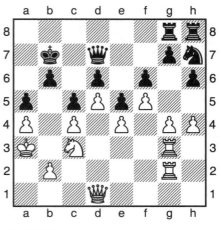

3) White moves

Five years later, Alekhine's great rival Capablanca put the idea to good use in a simultaneous display: 51 ♘e2 planning ♘g1-f3, ♕g1 and g5, opening the g-file and so cracking open the black position.

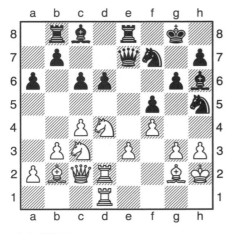

4a) White moves

From one of the author's games. 19 e4 seemed premature due to 19...♘xf4!? 20 gxf4 ♗xf4+, with troubling counterplay. Preparation is needed: 19 ♖e2! ♕f8 20 ♖de1 ♗g7 21 ♕d2! ♘f6 *(4b)*.

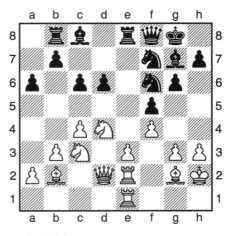

4b) White moves

White's major pieces are now much better placed to support the central advance, and his king is safer than it was a few moves ago. Finally 22 e4! gives White powerful pressure on the central files.

An Exposed King

The king needs continuous protection

The most important strategic factor of all is king safety. It doesn't matter what other strategic gains you have made; if your king is in danger, it can outweigh everything else, and this is true in all phases of the game.

One of our first goals in the opening is to protect the king by castling, which can be accomplished as early as move 4. However, there are often good strategic reasons for delaying castling, in which case we must be alert to any dangers the king faces in the centre. Dangerous situations can also arise when we have castled, especially if the king is exposed by weakening pawn moves or by a lack of piece defence. If a castled position becomes too unsafe, it may make sense to evacuate the king to the other wing. This long trek takes time and may be perilous in itself, but is sometimes the best way to consolidate an advantage. It is important for the king to flee before it is too late. An instructive example is Romanovsky-Vilner, USSR Ch, Moscow 1927 (diagram 4a).

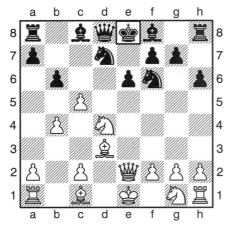

1) Black moves

In the game Murei-Gelfer, Ramat Hasharon 1980, Black played the suicidal move 12...bxc5?? and resigned after 13 ♘c6. He had forgotten about his king after 13...♕c7 14 ♕xe6+!! fxe6 15 ♗g6#.

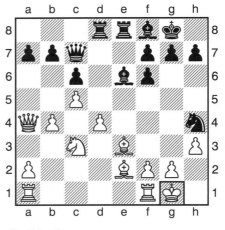

2) Black moves

In T.Ernst-K.Berg, Malmö 1988 Black lashed out 17...♗xh3!. Since it is not possible to protect g2 and 18 gxh3 fails to 18...♖xe3 19 fxe3 ♕g3+ 20 ♔h1 ♕g2#, Ernst decided to resign.

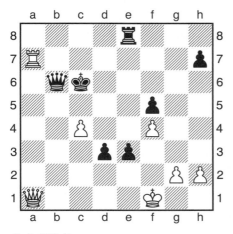

3a) White moves

41 ♕a4+ ♔d6 42 c5+! ♔xc5 43 ♕a3+ ♔c6 44 ♕c3+ wins since the d-pawn falls with check and the black king remains fatally exposed. Rellstab-Richter, German Ch 1938 saw 41 ♖a6?? *(3b)*.

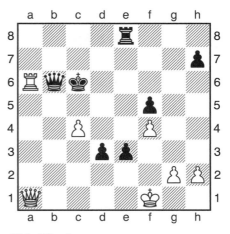

3b) Black moves

After 41...e2+ 42 ♔e1 d2+ 43 ♔xd2 e1♕+ 44 ♔xe1 ♖d8+! (White had missed this *zwischenzug* – i.e. 'in-between' move) 45 ♔c3 ♕xa6 Black won with his extra rook. The white king proved too weak.

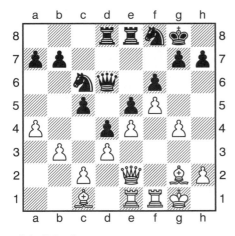

4a) Black moves

With 26...♔f7 the king flees to the queenside. 27 g5 ♔e7 28 ♖f3 ♔d7 29 ♖g3 ♔c8 30 gxf6 gxf6 31 ♗f3 ♘d7 32 ♕g2 a5 33 ♗h5 ♖e7 34 ♖g8 ♘b6 35 ♗h6 ♖c7 36 ♖d1 ♘b4 37 ♖d2 *(4b)*.

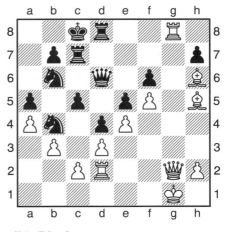

4b) Black moves

The journey is not over: after 37...♔b8 38 ♕g3 ♔a7 the king is safer but White won anyway after 39 ♖g2 ♘c8 40 ♕f2 ♘c6 41 ♖2g3 ♔a6 42 ♕g2 (Alekhine's Gun) 42...♖cd7 43 ♗e8 ♖c7 44 ♗f8.

SMART STRATEGY 34 · The King's Fortress

There are different ways of protecting the king

Castling should not be an automatic decision, as it is an important strategic decision. The king should be protected from danger, but its location should also be in harmony with our longer-term plans. For instance, if the best plan in the position is a kingside pawn advance, then it is best if we haven't already castled kingside.

Basically there are four options for the king: castle kingside, castle queenside, castle 'by hand' or not to castle at all. We have already seen many examples of the most common option, kingside castling. In some openings queenside castling is appropriate because it brings a rook quickly to the centre and allows a kingside pawn-storm. Castling 'by hand' is normally done if the king has already had to move: we then 'walk' the king over to one wing or the other. This may have the advantage of leaving the rook free to operate on the h-file. Occasionally the king will be safest in centre, generally in openings where the centre pawns still provide a defensive shell on their second or third ranks. Sometimes there is no rush to make a castling decision, and it may be more important to bring a piece to a better square, as in diagram 2.

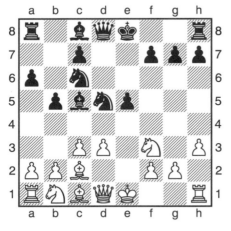 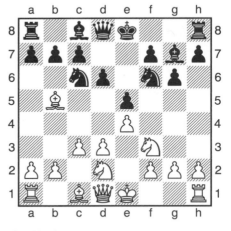

1) Black moves

White plans to open the e-file by playing d4, so both sides need to castle quickly. After 9...0-0 10 0-0 h6 11 d4 exd4 12 cxd4 ♗b6 the game is about even.

2) White moves

The position is closed and the priority is to bring the pieces to their best squares. White launches an attack by 7 ♘f1 0-0 8 ♗a4 ♘d7 9 ♘e3 ♘c5 10 ♗c2 ♘e6 11 h4!.

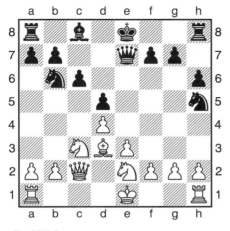

3) White moves

It is normally safest for Black to castle the same side as White; e.g., 12 0-0 0-0. After 12 0-0-0 Black must decide between 12...0-0, leading to sharp play, or the quieter 12...♗e6 13 ♔b1 0-0-0.

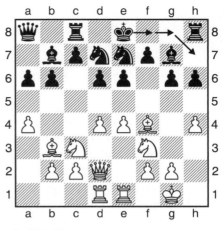

4) Black moves

The pressure on h6 prevents Black from castling normally but with 15...♔f8 16 ♕e2 ♔g8 17 ♘b1 ♔h7 18 c3 ♖hf8 Black had safely castled 'by hand' in Blauert-Lau, West German Ch 1989.

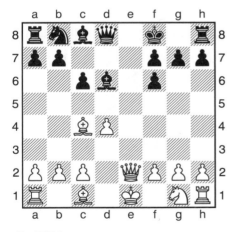

5) White moves

Black is preparing to castle 'by hand' with ...h5, ...g6 and ...♔g7. White prevents this set-up by 8 ♕h5! g6 9 ♗h6+ ♔g8 10 ♕f3, with some advantage. The king has 'castled' but the h8-rook hasn't!

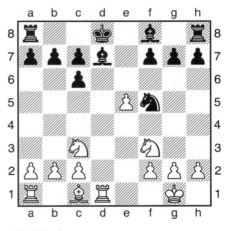

6) Black moves

Black has lost the right to castle because of an early exchange of queens on d8. After 10...♔c8 11 ♘g5 ♗e8 12 b3 b6 13 ♗b2 ♗e7 14 ♘ge4 ♔b7 15 ♖d3 ♖d8 16 ♖ad1 ♔c8 Black has castled 'by hand'.

SMART STRATEGY **35**

The Active King

The king is stronger than a minor piece!

In the endgame it is very important for the king to play an active role. In a simplified position where there is little danger of a mating attack, the king *must* be used as a fighting piece. As an active unit the king is reckoned to have a value of 4 'pawns' – more than a minor piece (3) but less than a rook (5). Of course, this doesn't mean that you can ever 'exchange' your king! But it does suggest that an active king can outweigh a significant material advantage or other strategic pluses.

The right moment to activate the king is sometimes earlier than expected: it may be possible to use it actively in the opening and middlegame. Two famous examples are Short-Timman, Tilburg 1991 (diagram 3a) and Navara-Wojtaszek, Biel 2015 (diagram 4a). Navara even went so far as to put his king on h8 having started from f2! He was nicknamed 'King David' after this incredible king journey. But this has a 'don't try this at home' warning; in his preparation, Navara had checked this idea with the computer very carefully before daring to play it in a tournament game.

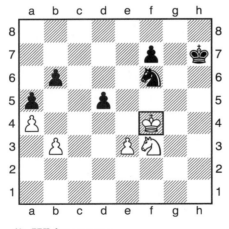

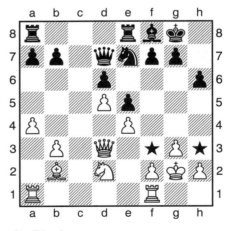

1) White moves

Aronian-Caruana, Stavanger 2015 went 42 ♔e5 ♔g6 43 ♘d4! (not 43 ♔d6? ♔f5 44 ♔c6 ♔e4), keeping the black king at bay. 43...♔g5 44 ♔d6 ♘g4 45 ♘c2 ♔f5 46 ♔xd5 ♘f6+ 47 ♔c6 and White won.

2) Black moves

Rubinstein-Duras, Karlsbad 1911. Black has just exchanged bishops on g2. But the white king is quite happy on g2, covering f3 and h3, and one step closer to becoming active in a later endgame.

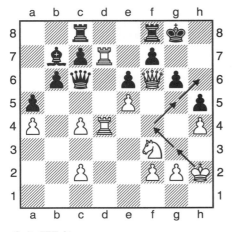

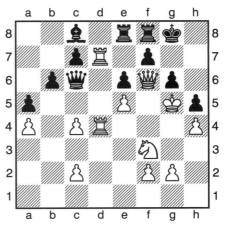

3a) White moves

Black is tied up but it is not immediately clear how White can turn the screw. Which piece can be improved? Short played the extraordinary king manoeuvre 32 ♔g3! ♖ce8 33 ♔f4! ♗c8 34 ♔g5! *(3b)*.

3b) Black moves

Timman resigned because of 34...♗xd7 35 ♔h6!, when White delivers mate on g7, while 34...♔h7 can be met by 35 ♕xg6+. White's marching king was safe because Black had no active pieces.

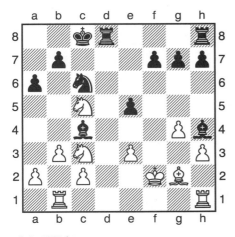

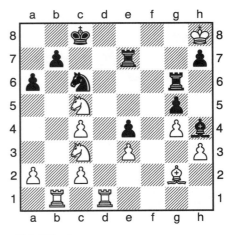

4a) White moves

White's unbelievable king activation begins: 21 ♔f3!? e4+ 22 ♔f4!? g5+ 23 ♔f5 ♖he8 24 ♖hd1 ♖e5+ 25 ♔f6 ♖g8 26 bxc4 ♖g6+ 27 ♔xf7 ♖e7+ 28 ♔f8 ♖f6+?! (28...♖eg7!) 29 ♔g8 ♖g6+ 30 ♔h8!! *(4b)*.

4b) Black moves

30...♖f6 31 ♖f1 ♗f2 32 ♖xf2 ♖xf2 33 ♖f1 ♖xg2? (33...♖e8+! 34 ♔xh7 ♖xg2 is correct) 34 ♖f8+ ♔c7 and now 35 ♘5xe4! wins. Navara played 35 ♘d5+? ♔d6 36 ♘xe7 ♔xc5 but won anyway.

Exchanging Material

Make exchanges only when they are in your favour

From Smart Strategy 10 we know that it is good to avoid piece exchanges when we have a space advantage and that when we are short of space, exchanges might helpfully free our game. But other things being equal, *making* an exchange of pieces is a concession: it is better to let our opponent make the exchange, as this tends to bring our pieces to better squares. This logic should be familiar from when we discussed pawn-tension in Smart Strategy 6.

So if we initiate an exchange, there needs to be a good strategic reason. Normally it is good to trade off pieces (not pawns) when we are ahead on material; heading for an endgame is often the simplest way to cash in an advantage. An exchange of minor pieces may be a useful way to deprive our opponent of the bishop-pair or to remove a good bishop or a strong knight.

Diagrams 1, 2, 4 and 6 show good exchanges while diagram 3 is a bad exchange. In diagram 5 it is a matter of taste whether the exchange takes place.

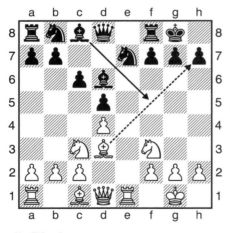

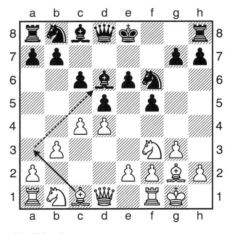

1) Black moves

Black uses the open c8-h3 diagonal to play 8...♗f5!, exchanging White's more active bishop. Note that the pin 8...♗g4? fails tactically: 9 ♗xh7+! ♔xh7 10 ♘g5+ ♔g8 11 ♕xg4, winning a pawn.

2) Black moves

White plans to exchange Black's good bishop with 8 ♗a3 but Black prevents it with 7...♕e7. After 8 a4 or 8 ♗b2 followed by 9 ♕c1, preparations are nevertheless made for the exchange to take place.

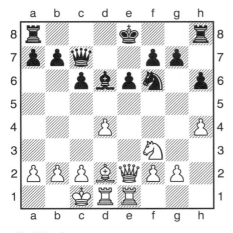

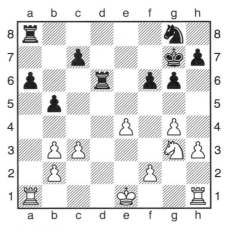

3) Black moves

15...♗f4?! exchanges a good bishop for White's worse one. 16 ♘e5! ♗xd2+ (16...♗xe5?! 17 dxe5 ♘d5 18 ♕g4 and 19 c4) 17 ♖xd2 gave White the advantage in Spielmann-Capablanca, New York 1927.

4) White moves

Capablanca-Baird, New York 1911 continued 24 ♖d1!, exchanging a set of rooks to reduce Black's counterplay and exploit the extra pawn. After 24...♖ad8 25 ♖xd6 ♖xd6 26 ♔e2 White went on to win.

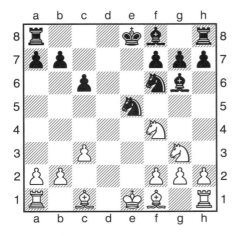

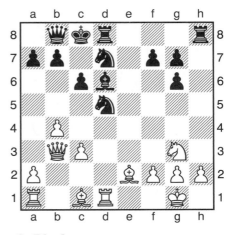

5) White moves

12 ♘xg6 hxg6 is rather an equal trade: the bishop was strong, but the half-open h-file is useful. If instead 12 ♗e2 Black can preserve the bishop with 12...♗c2!? followed by ...h6.

6) Black moves

Jon Ludvig Hammer, Carlsen's assistant, made a good exchange here: 16...♗xg3! 17 fxg3 (a forced weakening due to the h-file play after 17 hxg3? ♕e5 18 ♗g4 f5 19 ♗f3 ♖h7!), when 17...♕c7! is best.

Weak and Strong Squares

Seek out the holes and force new ones too

If you have a weak square (also known as a 'hole'), then it is also a strong square for the opponent. What is a hole? It's a square in your half of the board that you can't protect with a pawn. Some weak squares are more important than others. The expression 'a weakness is only a weakness if it can be exploited' is worth bearing in mind. Weak squares near the king are especially serious, while a hole that allows an enemy knight to plant itself firmly on a central square is generally a major problem. A famous example of a hole near the king being exploited to devastating effect is Steinitz-Blackburne, London 1876 (diagram 3a).

Sometimes we find a *complex* of several weak squares of a particular colour. This happens because of a damaged pawn-structure or due to the exchange of a bishop that covered those squares. Again we turn to Steinitz – the first world champion and a great strategist – for an example. In Steinitz-Sellman, Baltimore 1885 (diagram 4a) he showed how to exploit a dark-square weakness.

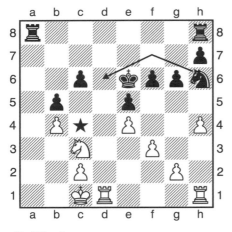

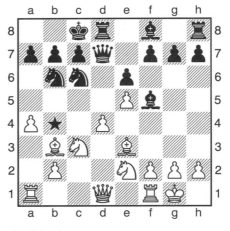

1) Black moves

White has just played the anti-positional 20 b4? instead of 20 b3. After 20...♘f7! White could not prevent the manoeuvre ...♘d6 followed by ...♘c4 with a strong knight cemented on the weak c4-square.

2) Black moves

White has just played 11 a4, intending a5. However, this weakens the pawn-structure (11 a3 is more sensible). 11...♗b4! occupies the hole and brings White's attacking plans to a halt.

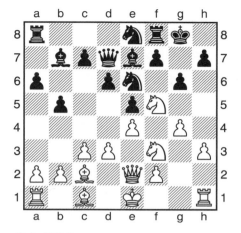

3a) White moves

Steinitz has provoked the weakening ...g6. Now it is a good idea to exchange the dark-squared bishop, as it could potentially cover the weak squares h6 and f6. So 15 ♘xe7+ ♕xe7 16 ♗e3 followed.

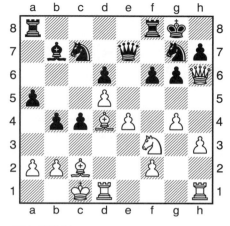

3b) White moves

Seven moves later Steinitz has occupied h6, and f6 is under pressure. After 24 g5! f5?! 25 ♗f6 ♕f7 26 exf5 gxf5 (or 26...♘xf5 27 ♗xf5 gxf5 28 g6) 27 g6! ♕xg6 28 ♗xg7 he won a piece.

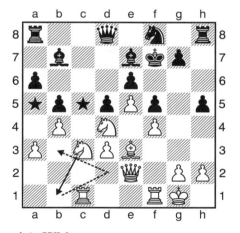

4a) White moves

The first weak squares to target are a5 and c5. Steinitz played 20 ♘b1! g6 21 ♘d2 ♘d7 22 ♘2b3 ♖c8 23 ♘a5, occupying the weak complex of dark squares while controlling the light squares.

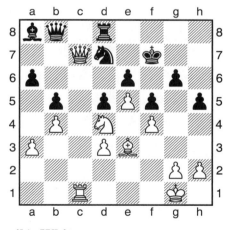

4b) White moves

White has invaded the seventh rank and now it is time to penetrate the complex of weak squares on the kingside by 30 ♗f2! and ♗h4. This was enough to make Black's fragile position crumble.

Piece-Activity

The most important of all smart strategies

The ultimate aim of almost any strategy is to make our pieces more active than the opponent's pieces. We control the centre so that we can eventually put pieces in the centre, where they will be very active. We carve out strong squares for our pieces so that they can sit unchallenged in locations where they can assist with active plans. If we are to win games, it is vital that, one way or another, our pieces function better than our opponent's pieces.

However, pure piece-activity is also a strategic theme in its own right. We might improve pieces already in play, as in diagram 1a. We might exchange our passive pieces for the opponent's active ones (diagram 2). In Smart Strategy 2, about development, we discussed the importance of having more pieces in play than our opponent, but activity is actually something to think about in all phases of the game. Active piece-play is often more important than material considerations, and is closely linked to the initiative. A famous example is diagram 3a (from Capablanca-O.Bernstein, San Sebastian 1911), where White made a highly unclear sacrifice of two pawns for activity.

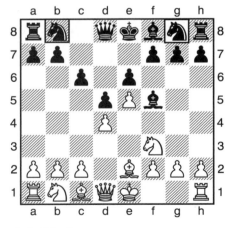

1a) Black moves

Rather than mechanically placing his knights on d7 and e7 (developed but passive), Black can go for maximum activity with 5...c5 6 0-0 ♘c6 7 ♗e3 ♗g4!? *(1b)*.

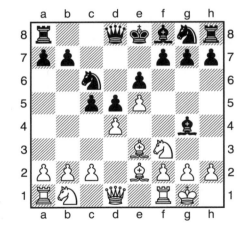

1b) White moves

Black has moved both the c-pawn and his bishop twice so that his knights can find good squares. After 8 c3 ♘ge7 9 ♘bd2 ♘f5 his minor pieces are actively placed.

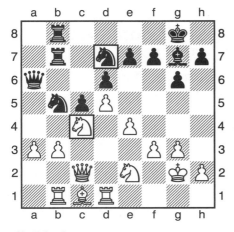

2) Black moves

Black's knight is passive on d7 so it makes sense to exchange it for the active c4-knight by either 20...♞b6 or 20...♞e5. With all Black's pieces active, he can expect full compensation for the pawn.

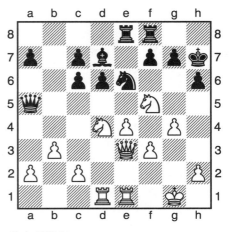

3a) White moves

Capablanca sacrificed two pawns with 22 ♞e2!?, the idea being to bring the knight to the very active square h5 via g3: 22...♛xa2 23 ♞eg3 ♛xc2. In practice at least, Black's defensive task is difficult.

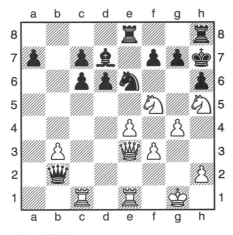

3b) White moves

Capablanca has achieved his dream position and played 26 ♖e2 ♛e5 27 f4 (the queen has to leave the a1-h8 diagonal) 27...♛b5 28 ♞fxg7!. If now 28...♞xg7 then 29 ♞f6+ ♚g6 30 ♞xd7 *(3c)*.

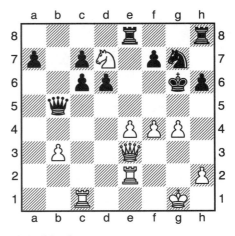

3c) Black moves

Black's king has problems and White's d7-knight is tremendously active. White threatens 31 f5+ followed by 32 ♞f6#. After 30...f6 White's whole position becomes active with 31 e5!.

Harmony and Coordination

*The value of the pieces increases when
they are working together in harmony*

By placing our pieces so they complement each other, we make them all more effective.
The bishop-pair is the perfect example, though it takes a little more effort to create such
harmony between the other pieces.

Let's look at harmony in the context of pawns. If they are side by side, they control
different colours and help the position as a whole because there are more plans available
with such a set-up. Compare it with two pawns attacking the same square; this is primar-
ily an attacking formation. Likewise we have a defensive set-up when a pawn defends
another pawn. Similar considerations apply to pieces. Imagine two knights one square
apart (e.g., c3 and d3); like a bishop-pair, they attack totally different networks of
squares, with no overlap. We can only appreciate harmony if we also understand disharmony. In Smart Strategy 22, we discussed the 'superfluous' piece, where two pieces are
in each other's way. This is almost pure disharmony: either piece would have good prospects on its own; their only weakness is their discord.

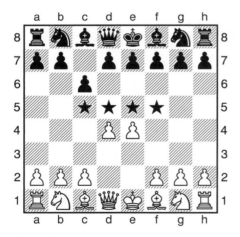

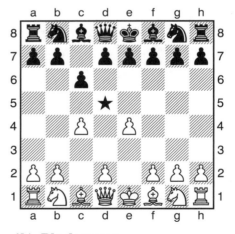

1a) Black moves

After the opening moves 1 e4 c6 2 d4
harmony is instantly achieved because the
two pawns control four different squares.
This means that White has more options
in his choice of future plans.

1b) Black moves

1 e4 c6 2 c4 is an attacking formation,
focusing on the d5-square. After 2...d5 3
exd5 cxd5 4 cxd5 ♘f6 5 ♘c3 ♘xd5 harmony is established with either 6 d4 or 6
♘f3, concentrating on the dark squares.

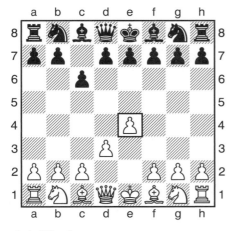

1c) Black moves

1 e4 c6 2 d3 is a defensive formation concentrating on reinforcing the e4-pawn. Play might continue 2...d5 3 ♘d2 e5 and harmony is established with 4 ♘gf3 ♗d6 5 g3 and so forth.

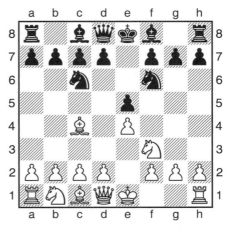

2) White moves

The developed knight and bishop control different colours and are in harmony. 4 ♘g5 is an attacking move concentrating on the f7-point, while 4 d3 followed by ♘c3 harmonizes with the f3-knight.

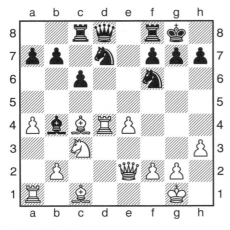

3a) Black moves

After 15...♕e7?! 16 ♗f4 ♗c5?! (better is 16...♖fe8!) White can prepare to place both his rooks on the central files with 17 ♖d2 followed by doubling with 18 ♖ad1. Black should prefer 15...♗c5 *(3b)*.

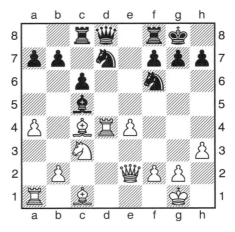

3b) White moves

The rook-lift 16 ♖d3 ♕e7 17 ♗a2 ♘e5 18 ♖g3 is less effective here after 18...♘g6, so White must play 16 ♖d1 and after 16...♕e7 17 ♗a2 ♖cd8, intending ...♖fe8 or ...♘e5, the game is equal.

Positional Pawn Sacrifices

The most common type of sacrifice

The pawn is the 'cheapest' and most plentiful unit in our army, and therefore the easiest to sacrifice in return for positional gains. One type of pawn sacrifice has a special name: a gambit is a pawn sacrifice early in the opening, generally in return for quick development and central control.

A reliable way to respond to a gambit, especially of a centre pawn, is to accept it and then, if necessary, give it back at a later stage to free one's game. A good example is in the Danish Gambit where White sacrifices two pawns by 1 e4 e5 2 d4 exd4 3 c3 dxc3 4 ♗c4 cxb2 5 ♗xb2. In positions 1a and 1b we shall see how in Mieses-Maroczy, Monte Carlo 1903 the solid player with the black pieces countered this dangerous plan. In Bronstein-Beliavsky, Erevan 1975 (diagram 2a) White shut an enemy piece out of the game by sacrificing his f-pawn. The 'cheapest' pawn to sacrifice is a rook's pawn, as this leaves fewest weaknesses; in Nimzowitsch-Capablanca, St Petersburg 1914 (diagram 3a) Black gained time and opened files on the queenside.

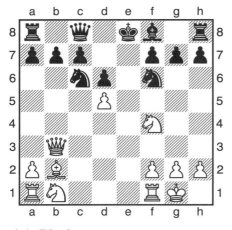

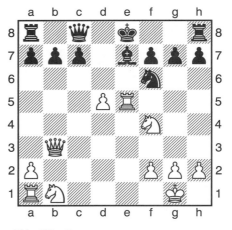

1a) Black moves

Maroczy, two pawns up, gave one back with 11...♘e5! (not 11...♘e7? 12 ♖e1) 12 ♖e1 (12 ♘d3 ♗e7 13 ♘xe5 dxe5 14 ♗xe5 is a better way to regain the pawn) 12...♗e7 13 ♗xe5 dxe5 14 ♖xe5 *(1b)*.

1b) Black moves

Maroczy offered up another pawn with 14...♕d7! 15 ♕g3? (also bad is 15 ♕xb7?! 0-0 followed by ...♗d6; White should develop with 15 ♘c3) 15...0-0-0 16 ♕xg7 ♕d6 and Black won.

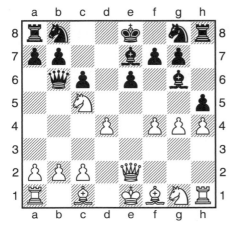

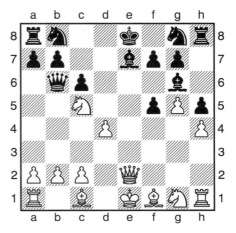

2a) White moves

The positional pawn sacrifice 10 f5! exf5 11 g5! *(2b)* is a clever way to restrict a bishop with the help of pawns (instead 11 gxf5? ♗xf5 12 ♗h3 ♗g4!! 13 ♗xg4 hxg4 14 ♕xg4 ♘a6 gives Black the advantage).

2b) Black moves

Can the bishop be kept out of play? After 11...♘d7 12 ♘b3 ♕c7 both players are fighting for control of the key f4-square. Now 13 ♗d2 prepares queenside castling followed by ♕f3, ♘e2 and maybe c4.

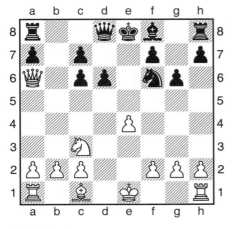

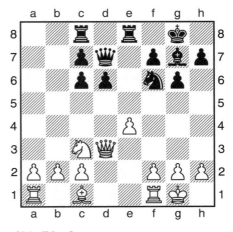

3a) Black moves

Capablanca sacrificed the a-pawn with 10...♕d7 11 ♕b7 ♖c8 12 ♕xa7, gaining time to develop. 12...♗g7 13 0-0 0-0 14 ♕a6 (14 f3 gives the queen a square on f2) 14...♖fe8 15 ♕d3?! *(3b)*.

3b) Black moves

White's queen no longer exerts pressure on the c6-pawn so Black prepared ...♘d7-e5-c4: 15...♕e6! 16 f3 ♘d7 17 ♗d2?! (17 a4 is preferable) 17...♘e5 18 ♕e2 ♘c4 19 ♖ab1 ♖a8 with positional pressure.

91

Do not be afraid to give up a rook for a minor piece!

A positional sacrifice is one made not for an immediate tactical payoff but based on an assessment of the longer-term prospects of the pieces left on the board. That is, a belief that our pieces will prove more powerful even though, by the standard way of measuring material, they are numerically inferior. An exchange sacrifice means giving up a rook for a minor piece. This is the second smallest material sacrifice after a pawn.

Exchange sacrifices were a particular speciality of Tigran Petrosian (World Champion 1963-9). His answer to the question about which is his favourite piece was "The rook, because I can sacrifice it for minor pieces!"

Normally the advantage of an exchange is decisive, so there needs to be significant compensation: a major positional plus and/or some material. For instance, a bishop, pawn and a weakened enemy kingside are normally at least full value for a rook (see diagrams 1 and 2a), while a strong knight on the fifth rank and a pawn may also prove sufficient (diagram 3a, one of the Lasker-Janowski match games from Paris 1909).

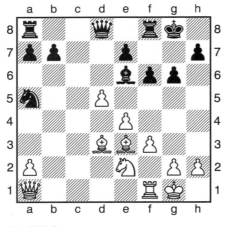

1) White moves

In one of the main variations of the Grünfeld Defence White has full compensation for the exchange due to his strong centre and Black's weakened kingside as well as the misplaced knight on a5.

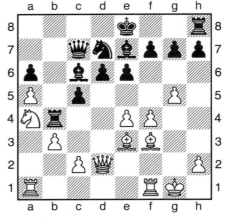

2a) Black moves

A good approach is 19...♗xe4 20 c3 ♗xf3 21 cxb4 ♗b7 followed by 22...♕c6, when White's king has problems on the diagonal. The young Petrosian played the exchange sacrifice 19...♖xe4!? 20 c4! *(2b)*.

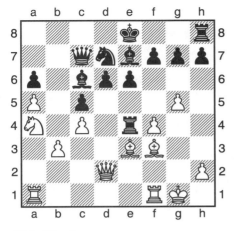

2b) Black moves

White prevents the rook from returning to b4 (instead 20 ♗xe4? ♗xe4 would have given Black a raking bishop). 20...h6! 21 g6? (21 ♕g2! is more resilient) 21...f5 22 ♘c3 ♘f6 23 ♗xe4 *(2c)*.

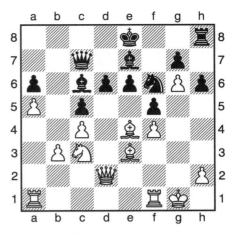

2c) Black moves

An interesting moment! Petrosian played 23...fxe4!? 24 ♖ad1 d5 and won thanks to his central pawn-mass. But 23...♘xe4! 24 ♘xe4 ♗xe4 is even stronger, keeping the long diagonal open.

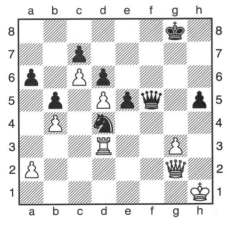

3a) White moves

Black has full compensation. 54 ♖a3? loses to 54...e4 55 ♖xa6 e3 56 ♖a3 e2, so play continued 54 ♖e3 ♕b1+ 55 ♔h2 ♕xb4 56 g4 h4! (keeping files closed) 57 ♔h3 ♕c4 58 ♕e4 ♔g7 59 ♔xh4 ♕f1.

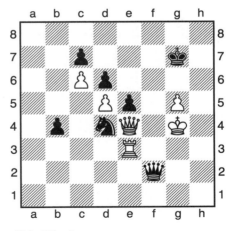

3b) Black moves

Janowski could now have won quickly with 65...b3! 66 ♖h3 ♕g1+ 67 ♔h5 ♕d1+ 68 ♕g4 ♕xg4+! 69 ♔xg4 b2 70 ♖h1 ♘c2 71 ♖b1 ♘e3+ followed by ...♘c4. The rook is clumsy without any open files.

SMART STRATEGY 42

Pawn-Breaks

Strive to have more pawn-breaks than your opponent!

The power of the pawns to shape the strategic direction of the game lies in *pawn-breaks*. In the simplest terms, a pawn-break is a move that offers an exchange of pawns. To put it another way, it creates pawn-tension (Smart Strategy 6).

But there is more to it than that. A pawn-break tends to be a latent idea in the position, a move that can be played at some point, but there is no rush. It can delayed until all the preparations are ready, and the tension it creates is *favourable*, i.e. the opponent's options for releasing it are unappealing. A well-prepared pawn-break may increase a space advantage or open key lines. Pawn-breaks are so important that if you have none it may be difficult to find a good plan at all. It is an advantage to have more pawn-breaks than your opponent since you can open the position in different areas of the board.

In the opening, pawn-breaks are a standard way to define the central structure. Later on, pawn-breaks usually arise on the wings.

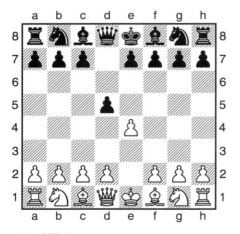

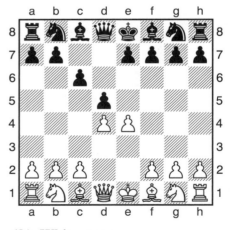

1a) White moves

A simple pawn-break can be seen after only one move in the Scandinavian Defence: 1 e4 d5. This attacks White's e4-pawn immediately, but 2 exd5 ♕xd5 leaves Black with no pawn in the centre.

1b) White moves

In the Caro-Kann Defence after 1 e4 c6 2 d4 d5 the central break is stronger since Black can maintain a pawn in the centre after 3 exd5 cxd5. The French Defence, 1 e4 e6 2 d4 d5, has similar aims.

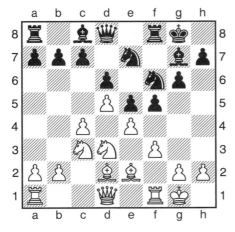

2) Black moves

Black has already used the pawn-break ...f5. Here it is normal to select a new target with 12...f4 followed by ...g5, preparing an eventual ...g4. White will go for a queenside pawn-break with 13 c5.

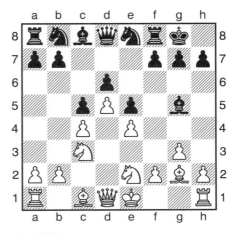

3) White moves

White can choose one of two breaks: attacking the e5-pawn with 9 f4 or after 9 0-0 ♗xc1 10 ♘xc1 ♘d7 11 ♘d3 g6 12 a3 play for b4, attacking c5. Black prepares the ...f5 break, attacking the e4-pawn.

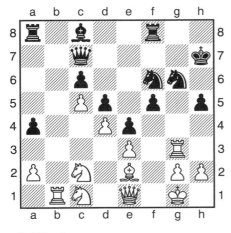

4) Black moves

White lacks pawn-breaks but Black can play one immediately with 26...f4. After 27 exf4 ♕xf4 Black has a protected passed e-pawn, good control of f4 and an open f-file. This is a lot from only one break!

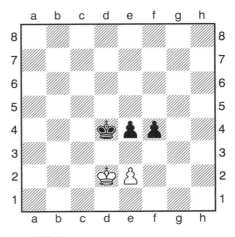

5) White moves

If Black were to move, he would win with 1...f3 since he can secure the opposition. With White to move, he draws with 1 e3+! fxe3+ 2 ♔e2 followed by 3 ♔xe3, with a standard theoretical draw.

Overprotection

Overprotecting key points gives your pieces freedom to move

Overprotection is a theme introduced by Nimzowitsch in his famous book *My System*. The idea is that important squares/pawns should be defended one more time than is strictly necessary. The point is that then none of these pieces are actually tied down to defending it – one of them can move away, and enough defenders remain.

For example, if an important central pawn is attacked twice and defended twice, then both defenders are tied down, and are prone to being overloaded, while lacking the freedom to carry out other tasks. Paradoxically, adding a third defender (overprotecting it) frees them all!

This is a remarkable insight from one of the greatest minds in chess history. It is also one of the aspects of Nimzowitsch's theories that has gained the least widespread acceptance, so if you understand it and use the idea wisely, you will have a significant advantage when you play others who do not understand it at all.

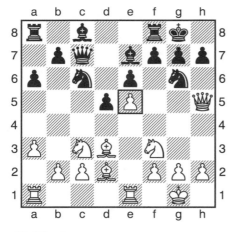

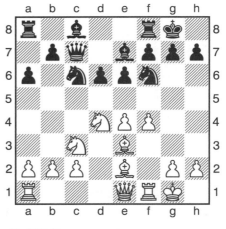

1) Black moves

Spielmann, while annotating the game Lundin-Kust, Stockholm Ch 1941, wrote that Nimzowitsch would have dreamt of putting the bishop on g3 and doubling his rooks on the e-file to overprotect the central e5-pawn.

2) White moves

11 ♖d1 overprotects the centralized knight. If Black exchanges with 11...♘xd4 White can choose either 12 ♗xd4 or 12 ♖xd4!? – overprotection provides more choice. If Black plays ...♘a5-c4, White can always reply ♗c1.

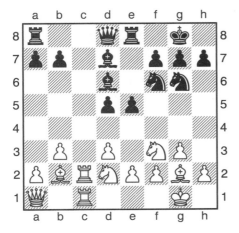

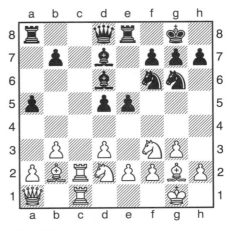

3a) Black moves

This is Réti-Yates, New York 1924. White plans 15 d4 e4 16 ♘e5 since e5 is merely 'protected'. Therefore Black needs to overprotect the important e5-square. He should first play 14...a5! *(3b)*.

3b) White moves

With this clever a-pawn advance, Black plans 15 d4 e4 16 ♘e5 a4 with strong queenside play. If White plays 15 a4, Black overprotects the e5-pawn with 15...♕e7, achieving a strong centralized position.

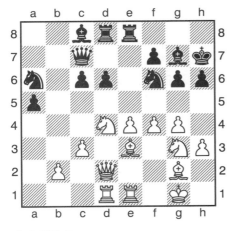

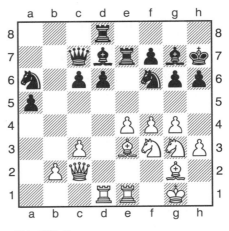

4a) White moves

Karpov-Timman, Montreal 1979. The overprotecting 22 ♕c2!? liberates White's minor pieces from the defence of e4. 22...♗d7 23 ♘f3 (preparing g5 and possible due to the queen move) 23...♖e7 *(4b)*.

4b) White moves

Seeing that ...♖de8 was coming, Karpov overprotected the e4-pawn even further with 24 ♗f2!?. With his centre secure, White can decide where and how to attack depending on how Black continues.

Play on the Wings

Concentrate your pieces on one wing

A *local superiority of force* is needed for an attack on the wing to succeed. Therefore it is a smart strategy to transfer pieces to one of the wings for the purpose of having more pieces in that area of the board than your opponent.

One typical device is to use the queen on the kingside while the opponent's queen is far away on the other wing. Such a situation is like temporarily playing with an extra queen. We saw a classical example in Smart Strategy 38: Capablanca-O.Bernstein, San Sebastian 1911, where Capablanca transferred two knights and a queen to the kingside while the black queen was on the other side of the board eating pawns. Here we shall look at the instructive game Petrosian-Chukaev, Vilnius 1951 (diagram 1a) where Petrosian did not even have to use the a1-rook because he did not need it! The last four snapshots (diagrams 2a-2d) are from the game Anand-Carlsen, Stavanger 2015 where Anand won by transferring all his pieces to the kingside and sacrificing an exchange (Smart Strategy 40!) in the process.

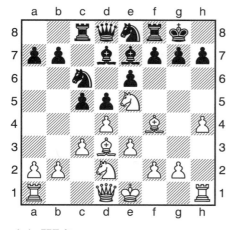

1a) White moves

With 11 ♘df3! Petrosian spent two moves bringing the queen's knight to the kingside. Black played 11...cxd4 12 exd4 ♘f6 and now a third move with 13 ♘g5 to provoke a weakness like ...h6.

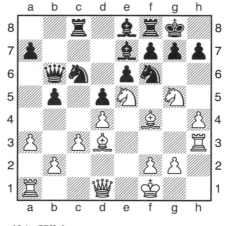

1b) White moves

A few moves later Petrosian used a rook-lift with 17 ♖g3! to provoke 17...g6 and after 18 h5 White was already winning. 18...♘xh5? obviously fails to 19 ♕xh5 gxh5 20 ♘gxf7+ ♚g5 21 ♖xg5#.

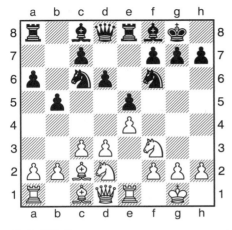

2a) White moves

Anand-Carlsen, Stavanger 2015 continued 11 ♘f1 g6 12 h3 ♗b7 13 ♘g3, when White had one extra knight on the kingside. 13...♘b8 14 d4 ♘bd7 15 a4 c5 16 d5 c4 17 ♗g5 ♗g7 18 ♕d2 ♖b8 *(2b)*.

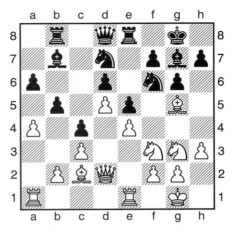

2b) White moves

19 ♘h2 ♗c8 20 ♘g4 ♘c5 21 ♘h6+ (occupying Black's h6-weakness) 21...♗xh6 (after 21...♔f8 22 axb5 axb5 the rook-lift 23 ♖e3 and 24 ♖f3 is good) 22 ♗xh6 gave White control of the dark squares.

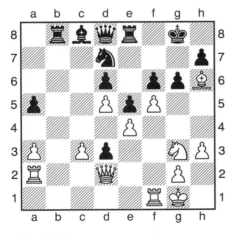

2c) White moves

Some moves later, Anand played 29 ♕d1!, to bring the a2-rook to the kingside (the greedy 29 ♕xd3 is met by 29...♕b6+ followed by ...♗a6, when White has lost the initiative): 29...♖e7 30 ♖af2.

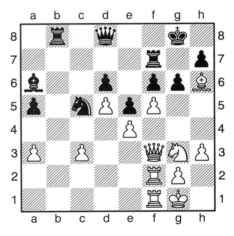

2d) White moves

What a picture of piece concentration! Anand played 33 ♕g4! g5 34 h4 ♗xf1 35 ♖xf1 ♕d7 36 hxg5 fxg5 and now the most convincing was 37 ♗xg5 ♔h8 38 ♕h4, bringing in the rest of the army.

<table>
<tr><td>SMART
STRATEGY</td><td>45</td><td colspan="1" style="text-align:right">Pawn-Majorities</td></tr>
</table>

SMART STRATEGY 45 — Pawn-Majorities

Create a passed pawn out of the majority

If we have a pawn-majority, it means that we have more pawns than the opponent in a particular sector of the board: the queenside, centre or kingside. The principal benefit of having a pawn-majority is that it may be possible to use it to create a passed pawn.

If both sides have a pawn-majority, then there may be a race to make a passed pawn, in which case a 2 vs 1 majority will tend to produce a passed pawn more quickly than a 3 vs 2 majority, etc.

The golden rule is to advance the *candidate first*. The 'candidate' is the pawn that has no enemy pawn on the same file in front of it. If we advance the wrong pawn, then our opponent may be able to slow our pawn-majority, or even stop it creating a passed pawn altogether. Generally it is better to have a pawn-majority that is further from the kings – generally this means on the queenside. However, our last example shows that activity can compensate for a queenside majority, particularly if it possible to control the only open file with a rook.

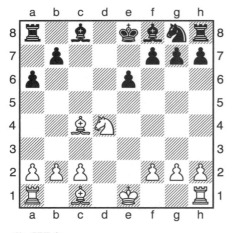

1) White moves

White has three pawns versus two on the queenside and Black four versus three on the kingside. With the kings in the centre, and neither majority very far advanced, no one has any real advantage here.

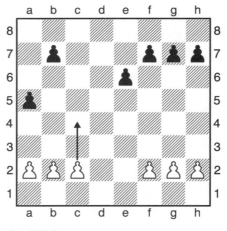

2) White moves

The correct way to create a passed pawn is 'candidate first' with 1 c4. After 1...b6 White plays 2 b3 (not 2 a3? a4!, when White's majority is crippled) followed by a3, b4 and c5, creating a passed pawn.

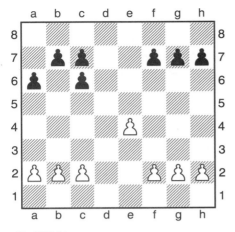

3) White moves

Black's majority is crippled. After the moves 1 c4 c5 2 b3 b5 3 a4 it is impossible for Black to produce a passed pawn. A set-up with pawns on c3, b2 and a3 also stops Black creating a passed pawn.

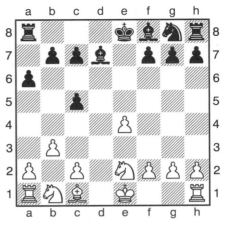

4) Black moves

Black can avoid a bad endgame by using the c-pawn actively. After 9...c4!? 10 bxc4 (Verlinsky-Alekhine, St Petersburg 1909) Black should play 10...0-0-0 with sufficient compensation for the pawn.

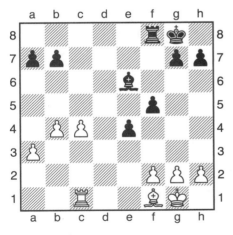

5a) Black moves

Yates-Alekhine, The Hague 1921 continued 25...♖d8!. The d-file control outweighs the queenside majority. After 26 g3 ♔f7 27 c5 ♔f6 all the black pieces were more active than White's.

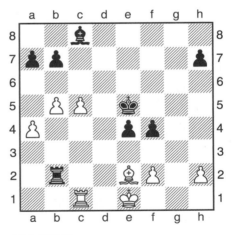

5b) White moves

By now Black's central majority is more dangerous: 35 c6 bxc6 36 ♖xc6? (36 bxc6! is necessary) 36...♗e6 37 ♗d1 ♖b1 38 ♖c5+ ♔d4 39 ♖c2 e3 40 fxe3+ fxe3 41 ♖c6 ♗g4 42 ♖d6+ ♔e5 and ...e2 wins.

Further Advanced Pawns

*It is not the number of pawns that counts
but how much of a threat they pose*

We have already seen how a *numerical* majority of pawns can create a passed pawn. But a *qualitative majority* can prove just as valuable: that is, better placed pawns. Sometimes the sheer degree of advancement makes the pawns a threat, especially when the opposing pawns are weakened in some way. An advancing body of two to four pawns can have a crushing effect. It's like facing a dangerous monster! This can apply at any stage of a the game: in the opening a mobile central pawn-mass can wreck the opponent's development plans. In the middlegame, a pawn-storm against the enemy king can lead to a devastating attack. And in the endgame it is most significant, as the pawns can force a queen, sometimes on their own, but especially with the help of the king or other pieces.

But be careful when pushing pawns forward. If the opponent can bring his pieces behind the advancing pawns, this could lead to a devastating counterattack, or leave the pawns themselves stranded and weak. Always use the pawns in harmony with the rest of the army.

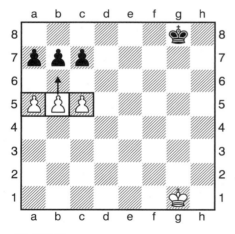

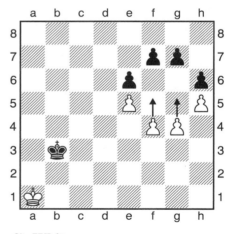

1) White moves

A famous pawn ending: a breakthrough by three pawns on their fifth rank vs three pawns on their back rank: 1 b6! cxb6 (or 1...axb6 2 c6! bxc6 3 a6) 2 a6! bxa6 3 c6 and the c-pawn queens.

2) White moves

This formation can also produce a passed pawn: 1 f5 (or 1 g5) 1...♚c3 and after 2 g5! exf5 3 g6 fxg6 4 e6 the pawn queens. Care is needed: 2 f6? gxf6 3 exf6 e5! allows Black too much counterplay.

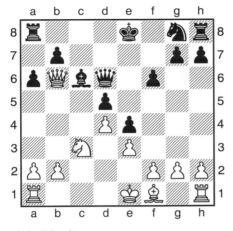

3a) Black moves

After 13...f5! the pawn is better placed than it was on f6, where it was in the way of the knight. 14 b4 sets White's queenside pawns in motion. 14...♞f6 15 ♕c5 ♚e7 16 ♗e2 g5 (*3b*).

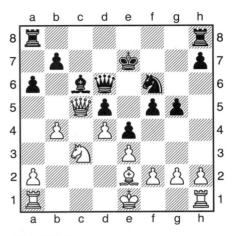

3b) White moves

Black prepares ...f4. With 17 a4 White does likewise on the queenside. After 17...f4 Black's kingside pawns give him domination in that area, while White's active play lies on the other wing.

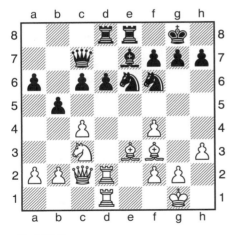

4) White moves

The pseudo-active advance ...b5 has made the f3-bishop stronger since it now puts pressure on the new weakness on c6. White can play the calm 18 b3, confident that Black has only weakened himself.

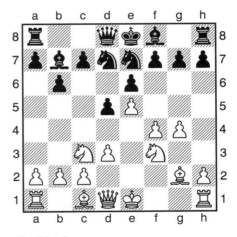

5) Black moves

White has advanced three pawns on the kingside. Black can reply 9...h5 10 h3 d4 and after 11 ♞e2 hxg4 12 hxg4 ♖xh1+ 13 ♗xh1 set his queenside pawns in motion by 13...c5, with chances for both sides.

The Minority Attack

The plan is to create a weakness in the enemy pawn-structure

After all we have said about pawn-majorities, it may come as a surprise to hear that it is sometimes a good idea to advance a pawn-*minority* as a way to attack a majority. Won't this just help the opponent create a passed pawn? Maybe; maybe not. The idea is to support the minority with well-placed pieces that reduce the majority's mobility, and then use pawn-levers to break up the enemy pawns. Even if they are passed, they will be static weaknesses. Our first two diagrams below show the idea in its purest form.

The most familiar type of minority attack arises in the Exchange Queen's Gambit (e.g., 1 d4 d5 2 c4 e6 3 ♘c3 ♘f6 4 cxd5 exd5), where there are fixed pawns on d4 and d5. The idea is not new; an early example is the game Steinitz-Lee, London 1899 (diagram 2), in which White advanced his a- and b-pawns against Black's a-, b- and c-pawns. White's main goal was to give Black a backward pawn on c6 by playing b5 followed by bxc6. In diagram 4a we see an example where White has been too slow with his minority attack, allowing Black to prevent it by placing a knight on the excellent square d6. Black then prepared his own minority attack on the kingside.

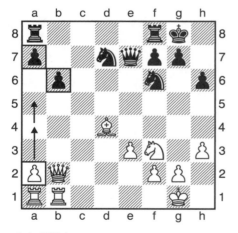

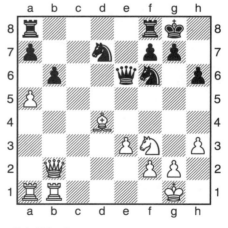

1a) White moves

1 a4! plans a minority attack on the queenside with one pawn vs Black's two by playing 2 a5 followed by 3 axb6. After 1...♕e6 2 a5 we have diagram 1b.

1b) Black moves

However Black recaptures on b6, he will be saddled with a weak pawn, on either b6 or on a7. The minority attack is a very potent weapon in such positions.

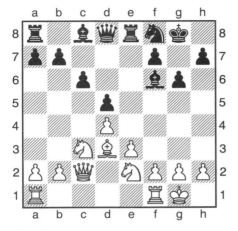

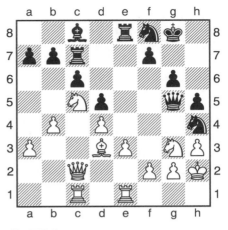

2) White moves

After 13 b4 a6 14 a4 ♗e7 15 b5 axb5 16 axb5 ♖xa1 17 ♖xa1 Steinitz had achieved his strategic goal: an exchange on c6 will leave Black unable to avoid a pawn-weakness of one type or another.

3) White moves

Black's kingside play must be respected. Here Karpov (World Champion 1975-85) ruined an ideal minority attack by 25 b5? ♘xg2! 26 ♔xg2 h4, with an attack. One preparatory move (25 ♗f1) was needed.

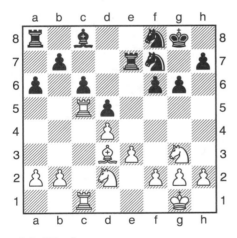

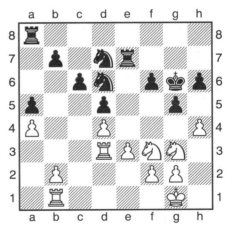

4a) Black moves

One of the author's games. My opponent played 20...♘d6 – a very strong location for the knight, halting White's plans on the queenside. After a dozen moves the position in diagram 4b was reached.

4b) Black moves

With 32...f5! Black played for a *kingside* minority attack. After 33 b4?! axb4 34 ♖xb4 f4 Black had a clear advantage. 33 ♔f1 f4 34 exf4 gxf4 35 h5+ ♔g7 36 ♘e2 is a better defence.

An attack on the flank is much more effective with a solid centre

A traditional theme in chess strategy is that a premature attack on a wing is best met by a thrust in the centre. This suggests that if the opponent doesn't have an effective way to strike in the centre, then we may well consider attacking on the flank.

The first world champion, Steinitz, provided some excellent examples on this theme. He would create a solid defensive central structure, such as placing pawns on e4 and d3. While the centre isn't fully blocked, it is nevertheless hard for the opponent to make any real breakthrough in the centre. We shall look at his first match-game against Blackburne in London 1876 (diagram 2a). Then in diagram 3a we examine a clever way for the defender nevertheless to attack the centre in this type of position. The reason Black manages to get strong counterplay in the centre is because he has placed his pawn on c5. Many of Steinitz's opponents did not understand how important this was.

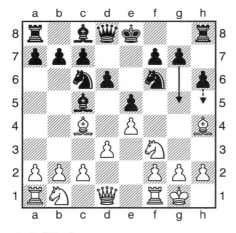

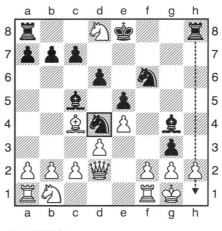

1a) Black moves

The fact that Black has not castled makes a striking idea possible: 7...g5 8 ♗g3 h5!. Steinitz's idea was to answer 9 ♘xg5?! with 9...h4! 10 ♘xf7 hxg3!? 11 ♘xd8 (11 ♘xh8 ♗xf2+ 12 ♔h1 ♕e7) 11...♗g4! 12 ♕d2 (12 ♘f7? ♖xh2) 12...♘d4! *(1b)*.

1b) White moves

Black's centralized knight is very strong. 13 h3 (13 ♘c3? ♘f3+ 14 gxf3 ♗xf3 leads to mate) 13...♘e2+ 14 ♔h1? (after 14 ♕xe2 ♗xe2 15 ♘e6 ♗b6 Black has no more than an edge) and now comes a pretty mate: 14...♖xh3+ 15 gxh3 ♗f3#.

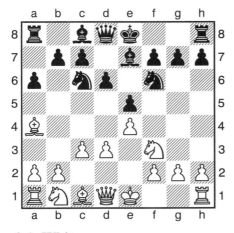

2a) White moves

With 7 h3 Steinitz prepared an attack on the kingside with g4. Blackburne continued 7...0-0 and with 8 ♕e2 Steinitz prepared to castle queenside. 8...♘e8 9 g4 brings us to diagram 2b.

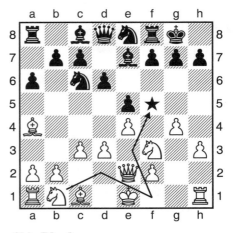

2b) Black moves

Play continued 9...b5 10 ♗c2 ♗b7 11 ♘bd2 ♕d7 12 ♘f1 ♘d8 13 ♘e3 ♘e6 14 ♘f5 g6?! (14...c5 is less weakening) 15 ♘xe7+ ♕xe7 16 ♗e3 ♘8g7 17 0-0-0 with an exciting battle.

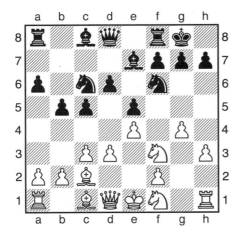

3a) Black moves

After 12...d5, 13 g5? is well met by 13...♘h5! 14 ♘xe5 ♘xe5 15 ♕xh5 ♗b7, threatening both ...c4 and ...dxe4 followed by ...♘d3+ – a strong central breakthrough. 13 ♕e2 d4 is diagram 3b.

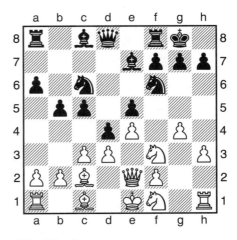

3b) Black moves

Black has counterplay in the centre and White's king is less secure. White must always be ready for possibilities such as ...dxc3 followed by ...b4, weakening the d4-square, or ...c4, opening the centre.

*When the opponent already has one weakness,
create another one!*

In many positions, exerting pressure against a single enemy weakness is not enough to secure victory. For each attack, the opponent is able to find a defence. It is a different story when manoeuvring against *two* enemy weaknesses, as alternating attacks can stretch the defence to breaking point. 'Weakness' should be understood in a broad sense; it might be a threat that the opponent must defend against, such as an outside passed pawn, the possibility of a rook penetrating on an open file, or an attack on a poorly-defended king (see diagram 3a, which is the from the final game of the 1927 world championship match).

When we have a space advantage, play against two weaknesses can prove especially effective, as we have more room to manoeuvre against the weaknesses. Diagrams 4a and 4b are from Blau-Keres, Zurich 1959. Estonian grandmaster Keres, one of the all-time greats, shows how to create an additional weakness in the opponent's position when the second weakness is not immediately at hand to exploit.

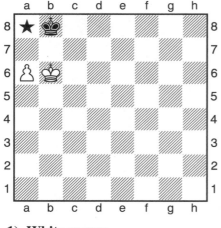

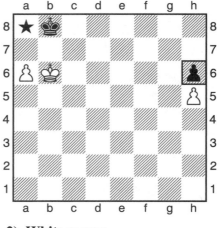

1) White moves

Here Black has only one 'weakness': the need to cover the pawn's queening square on a8. This is easily done: 1 ♔c6 ♔a7 2 ♔b5 ♔a8 or 1 a7+ ♔a8 2 ♔a6 and it is stalemate.

2) White moves

If we add a second weakness on h6, White can head for it with 1 ♔c6 ♔a7 2 ♔d6 ♔xa6 3 ♔e6 ♔b6 4 ♔f6 ♔c6 5 ♔g6 ♔d6 6 ♔xh6 ♔e7 7 ♔g7 and Black's king is short of the tempo it needs to reach f8.

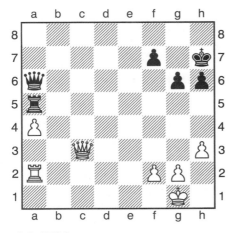

3a) White moves

Black's king is vulnerable and he must blockade the a-pawn. 40 ♖d2! threatens 41 ♖d8. Then 40...♖xa4? loses to 41 ♖d8 g5 42 ♕h8+ ♔g6 43 ♕e5!, while after 40...♕b6 41 ♖b2 ♕d8, 42 ♖b8! is strong.

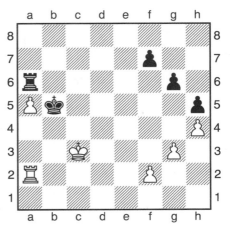

3b) White moves

Now the porous kingside is Black's second weakness, and 62 ♔d4! takes advantage. After 62...♔b4 63 ♖a1! ♔b3 64 ♔c5 or 62...♖d6+ 63 ♔e5 ♖e6+ 64 ♔f4 ♔a6 65 ♔g5, White will win the endgame.

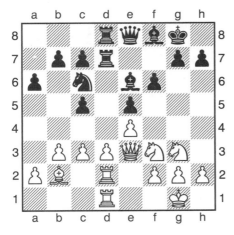

4a) Black moves

The d3-pawn is the first weakness. With 19...a5! Black targets the b3-pawn. Then 20 d4 cxd4 21 cxd4 exd4 22 ♘xd4 ♗c5 gives Black an annoying pin, while 20 ♘e2 a4 is diagram 4b.

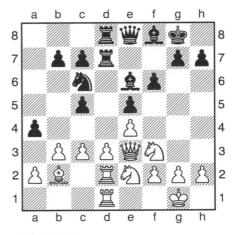

4b) White moves

Now 21 c4 weakens the d4-square, while 21 bxa4 was strongly met by 21...♗xa2!. The idea is that after 22 c4 ♗b3 23 ♖a1 ♘b4! Black threatens 24...♘c2, but 24 ♘e1 fails to 24...♗xc4.

109

Connecting Opening, Middlegame and Endgame

Think of the different phases of the game as only one phase

During the opening and the middlegame, we should spare a thought for how our decisions will affect our chances in the next stage of the game. For instance, if we are burning our boats going for an all-out attack in the middlegame, it might mean that most endgames will be hopeless for us. In that case, we should weigh the decision carefully, and be especially alert to ways that our opponent might engineer a queen exchange.

Just as accurate calculation is needed to implement our plans successfully, so strategic thinking is needed to be sure our plans are taking the game in the right direction. In this final section of the book we look at some specific examples where a long-term overview is vital. Diagram 2a shows a case where the possessor of an IQP is content to exchange pieces (contrary to the normal guideline) as long as the opponent is left with the 'wrong' bishop. In diagrams 3 and 4 a particular exchange should be avoided. Diagram 5 features the creation of a 'second weakness'.

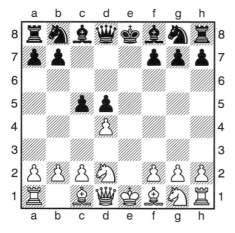

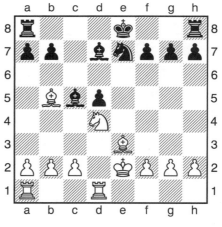

1) White moves

With an IQP about to arise, White wants to exchange minor pieces and queens. The variation 5 ♗b5+ ♗d7 6 ♕e2+ ♕e7?! (6...♗e7! is better) 7 ♗xd7+ ♘xd7 8 dxc5 ♘xc5 9 ♘b3 makes White happy.

2a) Black moves

Black can engineer the right exchanges of minor pieces by 13...♗xd4 14 ♗xd7+ ♔xd7 15 ♖xd4 – White's *dark-squared* bishop cannot attack the isolated pawn on d5. 15...♖hc8 16 c3 leads to diagram 2b.

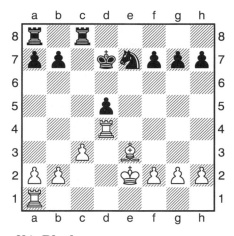

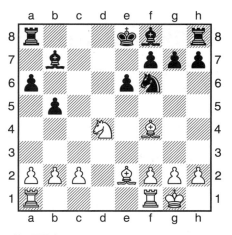

2b) Black moves

If White had wanted to prevent the exchange of rooks he could have played 16 ♔d3 instead. Now it is in Black's interest to play 16...♖c4! intending 17 ♖ad1 ♖xd4 18 ♗xd4 ♘f5! with equal play.

3) White moves

The exchange 14 ♗f3?! does not make sense since an attack on g2 is not a worry (with queens in the board it would be a different matter). After 14...♗xf3 15 ♘xf3 ♖c8 Black will control the light squares.

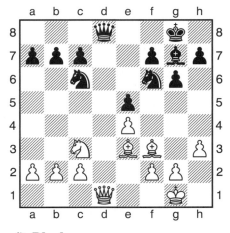

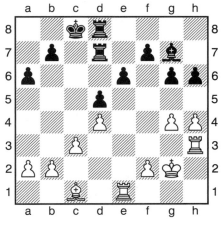

4) Black moves

Black should avoid the exchange of queens since after 17...♕xd1+?! 18 ♗xd1 White's strong light-squared bishop gives him the better ending. Better is 17...♘d4! 18 ♗xd4 exd4 19 e5 ♘e8.

5) White moves

White can improve his pawn position on the kingside with 29 h5 g5 30 f4 gxf4 31 ♗xf4, when Black has two weaknesses on h6 and f7. Also g5, creating a passed pawn, is a possibility.

Name the Strategic Concept

In the following diagrams, your task is to name the strategic concept that is shown by the arrows in each diagram. These are all concepts that have been discussed somewhere in this book. In some cases there is more than one idea involved. Each time you will be offered a choice of two options; select the one that best describes the main strategic theme.

Take 1 point for each correct answer.

The solutions will often provide some additional information or explanation. This is for your education and interest! So feel free to think about each position a little before looking at the solutions; you will learn more that way. But you do not need to have foreseen the game continuation or assessed the position to get credit.

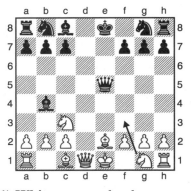

1) White moves: *development* or *bishop-pair*?

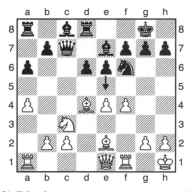

2) Black moves: *minority attack* or *pawn-break*?

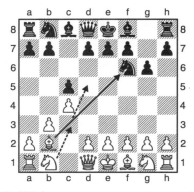

3) White moves: *outpost* or *exchange sacrifice*?

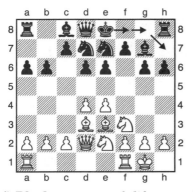

4) Black moves: *rook-lift* or *castling by hand*?

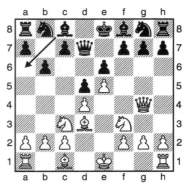

5) Black moves: *bad bishop/good bishop* or *centralization*?

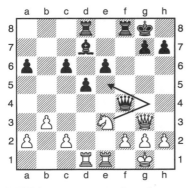

6) White moves: *isolated pawn* or *outpost*?

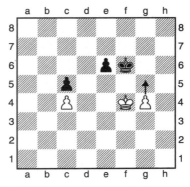

7) White moves: *doubled pawns* or *outside passed pawn*?

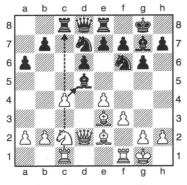

8) White moves: *open file* or *backward pawn*?

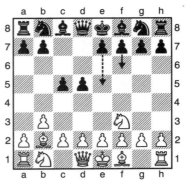

9) Black moves: *restricting a bishop* or *hypermodern development*?

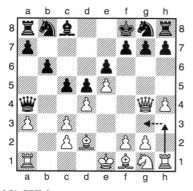

10) White moves: *pawn-tension* or *rook-lift*?

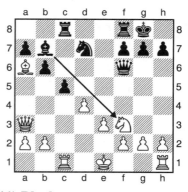

11) Black moves: *positional exchange sacrifice* or *the superfluous piece*?

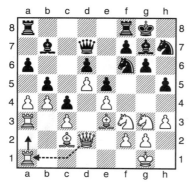

12) White moves: *overprotection* or *tripling on a file*?

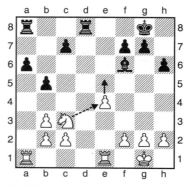

13) White moves: *centralization* or *isolated pawn couple*?

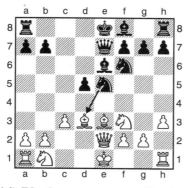

14) Black moves: *neutralization of the centre* or *bishop-pair*?

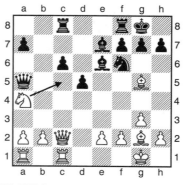

15) White moves: *blockading a pawn* or *crippled pawn-majority*?

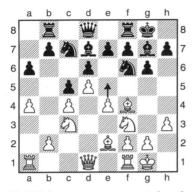

16) White moves: *principle of two weaknesses* or *pawn-break*?

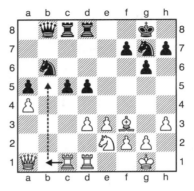

17) White moves: *occupying a weak square* or *undermining a pawn-chain*?

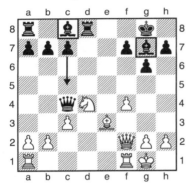

18) Black moves: *Steinitz restriction method* or *dominant knight*?

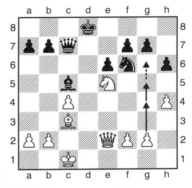

19) White moves: *little centre* or *minority attack*?

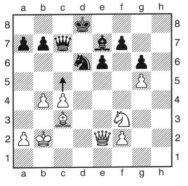

20) White moves: *candidate first* or *classical centre*?

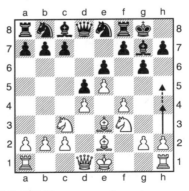

21) White moves: *hanging pawns* or *opening a file*?

Strategic Skills Exercises

In the following six positions, your challenge is to find the best move. This will be an idea based on a strategic concept that we have discussed somewhere in this book. The hint reveals where that was, and this may provide a clue to the right idea.

You are not necessarily looking for an instant checkmate or an immediate forced win, but in some of the positions such a possibility does exist. After all, checkmate is the ultimate strategic goal! But your focus should be on finding the best move, whatever it may be. You get 1 point for finding the correct first move in each case.

Target Scores

Once you have completed these exercises and the previous set, add up your points for an overall score out of a maximum of 27. Your score corresponds to your strategic ability roughly as follows:

26-27	**Master standard**
22-25	**Tournament strength player**
18-21	**Excellent Strategic Skills**
15-17	**Promising – join a chess club!**
12-14	**Good Strategic Knowledge**
9-11	**More practice needed**
6-8	**Read the book again!**
0-5	**You made some very unlucky guesses!**

SUPERFLUOUS KNIGHT

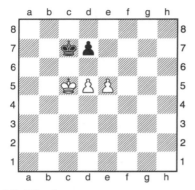

22) Black moves
Hint: see Smart Strategy 42

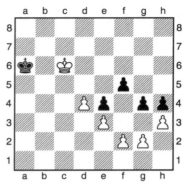

23) Black moves
Hint: see Smart Strategy 46

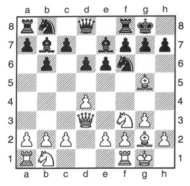

24) White moves
Hint: see Smart Strategy 24

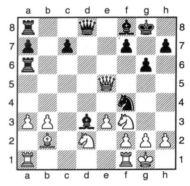

25) Black moves
Hint: see Smart Strategy 21

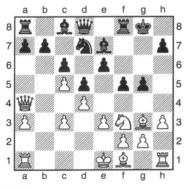

26) Black moves
Hint: see Smart Strategy 27

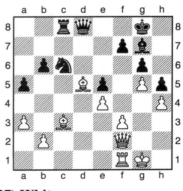

27) White moves
Hint: see Smart Strategy 29

Solutions to Test Positions

Name the Strategic Concept

1. Rapid **development** in an open position. In one of his match-games against Anderssen in Paris in 1858, Morphy played 7 ♘f3! ♗xc3+ 8 bxc3 ♕xc3+ 9 ♗d2 and got more than enough compensation for the pawn with his better development. These were the two leading players of the time.

2. A central **pawn-break**.
Following 13...e5! 14 ♗e3 exf4 White's pawn-centre is neutralized after either 15 ♗xf4 ♗e6 16 ♕g3 ♘d7 with control of e5, or 15 ♖xf4 ♗e6 followed by ...d5.

3. Doubling pawns and occupying a central **outpost**.
In Karpov-Browne, San Antonio 1972, 4 ♗xf6! doubled Black's pawns as well as weakening the d5-square. After 4...exf6 5 ♘c3 Karpov secured his grip on this square by developing the light-squared bishop on g2, supporting a knight on d5.

4. Castling 'by hand' (or **artificially**).
This could have arisen in a game Smirin-Hillarp Persson, Helsingør 2015. The pressure on h6 prevents Black from castling normally, so if he wants to place his king on the kingside, he must do so the slow way: with ...♔f8-g8-h7 and then move the h8-rook. This takes four moves instead of two (...0-0 and ...♔h7).

5. Exchanging a **bad bishop** for a good bishop.
With 7...♗a6 Black trades his bishop that is obstructed by his central pawns for White's bishop that has more freedom. After 8 0-0 ♘e7 9 ♘e2 ♗xd3 10 cxd3 c5 followed by ...♘f5 or ...♘bc6 Black has nearly equalized.

6. Occupying an **outpost**.
In Tal-R.Byrne, Moscow 1971, the tactical magician Mikhail Tal (World Champion 1960-1) played the excellent strategic move 22 ♘g4!. White's knight is very interested in sitting on the outpost on e5, where it has multiple functions. Most notably, it prevents the e6-pawn from advancing, which would open the c8-h3 diagonal for the bishop.

7. Outside passed pawn.
The passed g-pawn acts as a decisive diversion. After 1 g5+ ♔g6 2 ♔e5 ♔xg5 3 ♔xe6 the black king is too far from the critical squares. White collects the c5-pawn and queens his c-pawn.

8. Opening a file.
In this Maroczy Bind formation, White's strategy is normally to open the c-file as he is better placed to control it. After 17 exd5?! e6! 18 dxe6 ♖xe6 Black's rook puts pressure on the white bishops. 17 cxd5 is better. Now 17...e6?! 18 dxe6 ♖xe6 19 ♘b4 is advantageous for White

since he will occupy the a2-g8 diagonal with ♗c4.

9. Restricting a bishop with pawns.
This position arose in the sixth game of the Candidates match game between Petrosian and Fischer in Buenos Aires 1971 – by winning this match, Bobby Fischer qualified to challenge World Champion Boris Spassky. Fischer played the clever 3...f6!, when White had no good way to prevent 4...e5, which dominates the centre and stifles the b2-bishop. On his previous move, Petrosian should have played 3 e3 (instead of 3 ♗b2?!) so as to be able to answer 3...f6 with 4 d4 cxd4 5 exd4.

10. A rook-lift.
10 ♖h3! gives White attacking chances on the kingside. 10...♘e7 (pawn grabbing with 10...♕xc2? is far too risky in view of 11 ♗d3 ♕b2 12 ♖b1 ♕xa3 13 h5

with a strong attack after ♖g3) 11 h5 with somewhat the better chances for White.

11. Positional exchange sacrifice.
After 16...♗xf3! 17 ♗xc8 ♖xc8 18 gxf3 ♕xf3 19 ♖g1 ♖e8! Capablanca (White) was only slightly better in his fifth world championship match-game against Lasker in 1921. "An ordinary player would never have thought of giving up the exchange in order to keep the initiative in this position, which was really the only reasonable way in which he could hope to draw the game." – Capablanca.

12. Alekhine's Gun (tripling on a file).
24 ♖1a2! was played in the first Fischer-Spassky match-game at Sveti Stefan in 1992. White's plan is to triple his major pieces on the a-file by putting the queen behind the rooks. After 24...♖fc8 25 ♕c1! ♗f8 26 ♕a1! the feared 'Alekhine's Gun'

A WEAK SQUARE

was completed and Black had a tough time defending along the a-file.

13. Centralization.
In a simultaneous game from 1926, Capablanca played 18 e5 with the idea of activating the c3-knight on the central e4-square. 18 ♘d5? would obviously have failed to 18...♗xb2.

14. Gaining the **bishop-pair**.
Normally the player with an IQP wants to keep pieces on the board with a move such as 10...♘c6. However, in this situation 10...♘xd3+! 11 ♕xd3 ♕c7 is better. Black wins time, gains the bishop-pair and eliminates a potential attacker of the d5-pawn.

15. Occupying an **outpost** (or **blockading** an **isolated pawn couple**).
Black has an isolated pawn couple and wants to push the pawn to c5 to create the more strategically double-edged hanging pawns. In the game Polugaevsky-Khasin, USSR Ch, Baku 1961, White prevented

this with the blockading move 15 ♘c5, which kept a definite strategic edge.

16. Central **pawn-break**.
With 12 e5 White achieves his dream pawn-break in this type of 'Benoni' structure. It secures extra space and puts strong pressure on the d6-pawn. Black's own desired pawn-break with ...b5 has been neatly prevented by four white units.

17. Open file / weak square.
28 ♖b1! emphasized the weak b5-square. After 28...♕a7 29 ♖b5 ♘e6 30 ♖db1 ♖d6 31 ♘c3 White had a clear advantage in the game Agrest-Engqvist, Swedish Team Ch 2007/8.

18. Bishop-pair / Steinitz restriction
method.
Rosenthal-Steinitz, Vienna 1873 was the first game where Steinitz demonstrated his method for using the bishop-pair in an open position with a symmetrical pawn-structure. First 16...c5 17 ♘f3 b6 limits

United Pawns

120

the activity of White's minor pieces. The further 18 Ne5 Qe6 followed by ...f6 deprives White's knight of its last central outpost.

19. Kingside **minority attack**.
In the game Teschner-Golombek, Hamburg 1955 White started a minority attack with 22 g4!. White's plan is to create pressure on the kingside with g5, possibly followed by g6. The game continued 22...Ne8 (22...Ke8! is better) 23 g5 hxg5 24 hxg5 Bd6 25 Nf3 g6 26 b4 Be7 27 Kb2 Nd6 leading to the next test position.

20. Activating a queenside **majority**; **'candidate first'**.
28 c5 secures an advantage since White's queenside majority is mobile and dangerous, while Black's own majority is practically frozen thanks to White's earlier minority attack. 28 Kb3? would have been a mistake since Black can prevent the 'candidate' from advancing by playing 28...b6!.

21. Pawn-lever to **open a file**.
With a blocked centre, attacking on the kingside with 9 h4! is highly logical. The game Tarrasch-Charousek, Nuremberg 1896 continued 9...Nc6? (9...h5 was necessary, although 10 Ng5 secures a significant advantage) 10 h5 Ne7 11 g4 f5 12 hxg6 Nxg6 13 Bd3 h6 14 g5 Kh7 15 Qe2 Rh8 16 Qg2 c5 17 gxh6 1-0.

Strategic Skills Exercises

22. The pawn-break 1...d6+ enables Black to draw after 2 exd6+ Kd7, as the white

king must move away and after 3...Kxd6 it is a basic endgame draw.

23. Black's only chance is a pawn break-through by his qualitative majority, and he achieves this by 1...f4!. Both 2 exf4 g3 3 fxg3 e3 and 2 hxg4 f3 3 gxf3 h3 see Black promote a pawn, and meanwhile he is threatening both 2...f3 and 2...g3, which would be the answer to a move such as 2 d5 or 2 Kd5.

24. The open long diagonal and loose b7-bishop proved Black's undoing in Maiwald-Bockius, Bad Wörishofen 1994, which ended abruptly 8 Bxf6 Bxf6 9 Ng5! 1-0. 9...Bxg2 allows 10 Qxh7#, while Black loses a whole exchange after 9...Bxg5 10 Bxb7.

25. The queen is dominated by 17...Ne2+ 18 Kh1 f6. Despite looking well-centralized, the queen is trapped in the middle of the board!

26. In Caruana-Grishchuk, St Louis 2015, Grishchuk naturally played 12...f4 with the purpose of limiting the action of the dark-squared bishop. After 13 Bh2 e5 he was taking over the game.

27. This is from the 18th game of the Steinitz-Zukertort world championship match in 1886. 35 f4! increased the pressure against the f7-pawn, which is not only backward and weak, but the only defence the black king has on the a2-g8 diagonal. Black defended it with 35...Qd7, but after 36 f5 the pressure on Black's position was decisive.

Glossary of Strategic Terms

Backward Pawn – A pawn that cannot advance and cannot be guarded by a pawn. It may become a weakness, and if the pawn itself is not a weakness then the square in front of it may be.

Bad Bishop – A bishop that is obstructed by friendly pawns (especially centre pawns) that are fixed on squares of the same colour as those on which the bishop moves. For instance, if Black has pawns fixed on d5 and e6 (both light squares), then his light-squared bishop is his bad bishop.

Bishop-Pair – Having two bishops while the opponent does not (e.g. he has two knights or bishop and knight). It is an advantage in most positions as the bishops coordinate very harmoniously.

Blockade – Placing a piece on the square in front of a pawn and thus preventing it from advancing. A knight is a good blockading piece, especially on a central square.

Centralization – Placing pieces in the central area of the board. Most pieces, with the possible exception of the rook, benefit greatly from being centralized, as they can attack a larger number of squares and influence all parts of the board.

Centre – The four squares in the middle of the board: d4, e4, d5 and e5.

Classical Centre – Two pawns placed side by side in a phalanx on the fourth rank in the centre.

Classical Development – A plan of development based on occupying the centre. For instance, White might seek to put pawns on e4 and d4 and develop his pieces towards the centre.

Closed Position – One in which there have been no pawn exchanges in the centre. In such a situation it may be more important to manoeuvre the pieces to their best locations rather than to play for straightforward rapid development.

Coordination – Pieces working well together, in harmony with each other. The bishop-pair is always in harmony, while another example is two knights on adjacent squares, covering a total of 16 squares with no duplication of effort.

Correct Development – Development that is based around a good plan. Planless development can leave pieces poorly placed.

Development – Bringing pieces into play. But there is more to development than simply moving pieces off their starting squares – they also need to be contributing to our plans, controlling important squares and working well with our other pieces. In an open position, being able to develop more rapidly than the opponent can prove a decisive advantage.

Domination – If we dominate an enemy piece, we deprive it of the ability to move to any safe squares.

Doubled Pawns – Two pawns of the same colour located on the same file. The rear pawn may have limited mobility, making it a potential target. Doubled pawns may also devalue a pawn-majority by making it unable to create a passed pawn.

Exchange Sacrifice – A sacrifice of a rook (worth 5 points) for either a knight or a bishop (worth 3 points each).

Exposed King – A king that lacks pawn-cover or defensive pieces around it, making it vulnerable to enemy attacks.

Extended Centre – The sixteen squares in the middle of the board (c3-c6-f6-f3).

Fianchettoed Bishop – A bishop that is developed on the long diagonal after moving the g-pawn or the b-pawn one square forward. For example, if White plays g3 and ♗g2, this is called a fianchetto.

Flexibility – Keeping options for a variety of different plans.

Good Bishop – A bishop that is not obstructed by friendly pawns (especially centre pawns) that are fixed on squares of the same colour as those on which the bishop moves. For instance, if White has pawns fixed on d4 and e5 (both dark squares), then his light-squared bishop is his good bishop.

Half-Open File – A file on which there is a pawn of one colour, but not the other. For instance, if there is a black pawn on the e-file but no white pawn, then White has a half-open e-file. The major pieces can exert pressure along such a file. Often a half-open file is better than an open file because it is a one-way street, and this makes it harder for the enemy rooks to contest control of it.

Hanging Pawns – If White has pawns on d4 and c4, but no pawns on the b- and e-files, he is said to have hanging pawns. Both pawns may become weak in the endgame but they have dynamic potential in the middlegame, as either pawn might advance aggressively.

Heavy Pieces – The queens and rooks. Also known as the major pieces.

Hypermodern Development – Controlling the centre with pieces from a distance, rather than occupying the centre with pawns. For example, a black knight on f6 controls e4 and d5, as does a white bishop on g2.

Initiative – The ability to make threats.

Isolated Pawn – A pawn that does not have any friendly pawns on the neighbouring files. It cannot be protected by a pawn, and may require piece support. The square in front of the pawn may prove a good outpost for an enemy piece, as it cannot be driven away by a pawn.

Isolated Pawn Couple – A d-pawn on the fourth rank defended by a pawn on the c-file, with no friendly pawns on the b- and e-files. An advance by the c-pawn would transform them into hanging pawns.

Little Centre – When you have only one pawn in the centre, placed on its fourth rank, and the opponent has a pawn on the adjacent file but on its third rank. After 1 e4 e5 2 ♘f3 d6 3 d4 exd4 4 ♘xd4 White has the little centre.

Long Diagonal – The a1-h8 diagonal or the h1-a8 diagonal.

Major Pieces – The queens and rooks.

Majority – see Pawn-Majority.

Maroczy Bind – A set up devised by Maroczy, a great player from Hungary. The structure arises after 1 e4 c5 2 ♘f3 ♘c6 3 d4 cxd4 4 ♘xd4 g6 5 c4 followed by ♘c3, making it hard for Black to play ...d5. It gives White a space advantage but not necessarily the overall advantage. It can arise from many different move-orders and openings – the term refers to the pawn-structure rather than a precise sequence of moves.

Minor Pieces – The bishops and knights.

Neutralization – To reduce the effectiveness of a piece by opposing or exchanging it with a piece of the same type. For instance, a fianchettoed bishop on b7 might be neutralized by placing a bishop on g2.

Open File – A file on which there are no pawns of either colour. Queens and especially rooks love open files.

Open Position – One in which there are very few (or no) pawns in the centre. Speed of development is very important, and castling has a high priority.

Outpost – A square in the enemy half of the board that cannot be covered by an enemy pawn. Such a square is perfect for a knight, especially in the centre. Outposts on the outer files may be excellent locations for rooks.

Overprotection – A device formulated by Nimzowitsch. The basic idea is that if you defend an important point one more time than is strictly necessary, then it frees any one of the defenders to move away if there is another important task to perform.

Passed Pawn – A pawn that has no enemy pawns in front of it on the same file or an adjacent file. Only the enemy pieces lie between a passed pawn and promotion.

Pawn-Break – A pawn move that threatens to capture an enemy pawn and thereby change the pawn-structure. This is often a good way to free a position or, e.g., avoid a backward pawn.

Pawn-Chain – Diagonally adjacent pawns positioned on the same colour squares, creating a chain.

EXPOSED KING

Pawn-Island – A group of connected pawns of the same colour. It is generally an advantage to have fewer pawn-islands than the opponent, particularly in the endgame.

Pawn-Majority – A larger number of pawns than the opponent has in a particular area of the board. For instance, if you have three pawns on the queenside and the opponent has only two, then you have a 3 vs 2 queenside majority. An unweakened pawn-majority can in general create a passed pawn.

Perpetual Check – When one side can give check forever, it is a draw.

Phalanx – Neighbouring pawns advancing side by side.

Principle of Two Weaknesses – A game is not easy to win when the opponent has only one weakness. But when there are two, the winning chances are much greater, as the defensive forces can be 'stretched' by alternating attacks against the two weaknesses. In this context, 'weakness' should be understood very broadly, as a feature that poses a threat or difficulty for the defender.

Positional Sacrifice – A type of sacrifice that does not give any immediate tactical reward but is founded on longer-term positional considerations.

Pseudo-Sacrifice – A sacrifice that reaps an immediate reward. It may serve as a form of exchanging manoeuvre; for instance, after 1 c4 e5 2 ♘c3 ♘f6 3 ♘f3 ♘c6 4 e4 ♗c5 5 ♘xe5, if Black accepts the pseudo-sacrifice with 5...♘xe5 White wins back the piece by the fork 6 d4.

Qualitative Pawn-Majority – When our pawns on one wing do not outnumber the enemy pawns, but nevertheless have better prospects of creating a powerful passed pawn because they are further advanced or less weakened.

Rook-Lift – Bringing a rook into an attack by moving it along a rank in front of its own pawns.

Secure Centre – When the centre is solid (i.e. the opponent cannot quickly open lines in the centre), an attack on the wing is more likely to be successful.

Space Advantage – Controlling a larger area of the board than the opponent. This grants our pieces more freedom than the enemy units.

Superfluous Piece – When a piece cannot move to a good square because another of your pieces is already placed on that square. This problem applies to knights more than the other pieces. If the f3-knight wants to occupy e5 but the other knight is already placed there, the f3-knight is the 'superfluous piece'.

Tension – Pawn-tension is created by offering an exchange of pawns. This tension is maintained as long as neither side actually makes the exchange of pawns (or advances their pawn). After 1 e4 d5 tension is created between the pawns. A decision must be made about how to deal with the tension because otherwise Black will just take the e4-pawn.

Wedge – A wedge cuts the position in two. For example, a black pawn on f3 in front of a white pawn on f2 prevents a white rook on h2 from moving to a2. A wedge is particularly strong if it is near the king since it is easier to checkmate with the help of the advanced pawn.

Great Chess Strategists

One of the first great strategic players was the Frenchman François-André Danican **Philidor** (1726-1795), who coined the idea that 'pawns are the soul of chess'. He was the first to understand that the play of the pieces and pawns is interrelated throughout the game and that the mobility of the pawns must be preserved. He did not like to play 1 e4 e5 2 ♘f3 since the f2-pawn could not move, and preferred 2 ♗c4. His idea was to continue with a later d3 and f4 and exchange the f-pawn for the e-pawn and thus get pressure on the half-open f-file.

The American chess genius Paul Charles **Morphy** (1837-1884) revolutionized chess by the brilliance of his play. His most enduring strategic contribution was his understanding of the value of development. He also showed that the more open the position, the greater was the importance of rapid development. His ideas could clearly be seen in his match in Paris 1858 against another great player, Karl Ernst Adolf **Anderssen** (1818-1879). The main reason Morphy managed to defeat the great combinative player was that he understood it was important to bring *all* the pieces into play before executing an attack. Anderssen's play was more based on creating threats and seeking combinations, and he succumbed to Morphy's convincing positional play.

The next great strategist in chess history was the first official world champion, Wilhelm **Steinitz** (1836-1900). He scrutinized Morphy's games and came to the conclusion that Morphy's successes were founded on logic and strategic insights: his combinations did not appear out of thin air but were based on sound positional principles. Steinitz set out to classify the most important elements, such as: lead in development, occupation of the centre, weak squares, pawn-majorities, open files, the bishop-pair and so forth. Indeed, many of our 50 'smart strategies' were first classified by Steinitz.

The Cuban chess genius José Raúl **Capablanca** (1888-1942) was arguably the greatest positional player of all time, in the sense that he intuitively 'knew' where to put his pieces. Garry Kasparov has said that if you study 100 of Capablanca's games you will greatly develop your strategic ability and positional sense. I have studied his games closely myself with great pleasure as well as learning important positional ideas. Do not forget this great player!

Suggestions for Further Study

1) Play through a lot of games

Strategic skills can be developed by studying games by the great masters. The four discussed on the previous page deserve close study, as do more modern players, such as Smyslov, Karpov, Andersson, Kramnik and Carlsen, to mention just a few. Pick a game collection with good annotations and play through the games while trying to understand what is going on.

2) Read lots of strategy books

When you are finished with this book, there are many other good strategy books out there. Those by Pachman, Euwe, Beim, Réti, Nimzowitsch, Watson, Nunn, Dvoretsky/Yusupov and Gelfand can all be recommended.

My recommendation is that you read one book at a time and start with either Pachman, Euwe or Beim. Play through the games while reading the annotations. When you are finished with a general work on strategy, you can continue with books by Réti, which describe the strategic ideas chronologically by following important players in history. You are then ready for Nimzowitsch's *My System*. The first part is for beginners while the second part is on a higher level. You might then examine Watson's books on strategy, which take Nimzowitsch as the starting point and survey subsequent developments in modern strategic thought. Books by Dvoretsky/Yusupov and Gelfand are for the very ambitious player; do not start too early with their works, but once you are ready for them, they will prove rewarding. There are no short-cuts in chess. The only way to learn chess is step by step, so if it is too difficult you need an easier book. But remember that if you are to improve, the work must be at least slightly difficult!

3) Play lots of training games

You can try out and test what you have learned in training games against friends or computers. This is a fun way to improve your chess before the real competition takes place!

4) Play lots of serious games

The best way to test yourself is to play 'real' tournament games, preferably at a classical time-limit or at least rapidplay (rather than blitz or 'bullet'). It is important that you have enough time to think during the games so that you can draw upon the new knowledge you have attained by playing through games of the great masters or studying strategies.

Good luck with all your smart strategies!

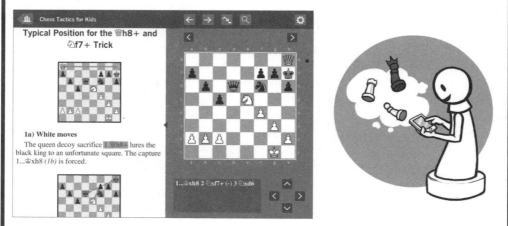